The Love Life Of Henry M. Naglee: Consisting Of A Correspondence On Live, War And Politics

Henry Morris Naglee

THE LOVE LIFE

OF

Brig. Gen. Henry *Morris* M. Naglee,

CONSISTING OF A

Correspondence on Love,

WAR AND POLITICS.

Edited by
Mrs. Mary L. *Schell*

186:.

6337.22
U.S. 6050.70

1876, May 2.
Minot Fund.
$0.90

INTRODUCTION.

In presenting this volume to the public, it may be proper to prefix a few words in apology. This seems necessary from the character of the correspondence, which is of that description one naturally supposes to be concealed among the shades of privacy, and which is better suited for the "loved one's" ear than for public examination. These letters would never have been published but for the pressure of circumstances. A suit for breach of promise was, some time since, instituted by the lady against the "General;" but her delicate and refined nature dreading to pass the ordeal of a public trial, she resolved to withdraw the prosecution, and (by the advice of friends) to publish these letters in vindication of the honesty of her cause. It is not our purpose here to discuss the principles contained in the accompanying correspondence. That the recipient was justified in believing the purpose of the writer to be honorable, none, we feel assured, can deny. The letters teem with sentiments of an affec-

tionate character. Their tenor is, in the main, of that
easy nature people adopt when corresponding with
those to whom they are, or anticipate to be, nearly
related. Indeed, many passages stress very strongly
on points of a marital nature, and which by all law,
" human and divine," an ingenuous and confiding
woman would be right in considering as an earnest
of promised marriage. It is unnecessary to speak
particularly of these passages, since the reader can
find no difficulty in their discovery, and, in sooth, their
number places them beyond the pale of our limited
space. Of the letters themselves, viewed with the
most good-natured eye, and bearing in mind the fact
that heroes are not always remarkable for their intel-
lect, we must admit that they are by no means of a
classic style of literature. It is true, that epistles intended only for *one* person are not expected to display
a very astonishing amount of ability. This is especially true of love letters, which are written, or sup-
posed to be written, under the wild impulses of passion,
and are therefore not to be compared to the disquisi-
tions of the same mind when not influenced by dis-
turbing emotions. This may in part atone for the
erratic style which the martial author is so prone to
follow in each of his amatory " sketches." His or-
thography was not as correct as we would have it, so
we took the liberty of making a number of judicious
corrections. Should any errors, therefore, appear in

the "spelling," they must be tacked to the compositor's and not to the "General's" reputation. His (the General's) style is, if we may use the expression, somewhat Pindaric, since he scorns, like that celebrated poet, all "rules but what himself ordains." He has a singular fecundity of words, and can reel out the most endearing terms of affection with the rapidity of a garrulous and practiced hand in the art of love. In short, these epistles bear the evidences of marked originality; and while they serve to throw a "little light" on his character, they also show what "bushels" of devotion he proposed to the fair recipient. These epistles—the accumulation of years—have ever been regarded by the lady to whom they were addressed, as the sacred mementoes of the man upon whom she had trusted with such certain, but alas! unrequited affection. It was with a struggle she consented to have them made public, and then only when it became imperative for her to defend herself from the calumnies of purchased miscreants. She has endured poverty, reproach and privation, rather than compromise the reputation of the man she loved, notwithstanding their publication would have secured her ample means, and this too while the "amatory penman" was rioting in the enjoyment of superabundant wealth. Yet these tender missives remained locked in secret, bedewed mayhap with many a tear, while Slander sent its hydra hiss abroad, and the faithless hero mocked at the ruin he had caused. Forbearance at length ceased to be a virtue; and this volume is made public that all may read of what a "grievous wrong hath been done in the land." Aside from their amatory character, these epistles are invested with many principles of social and political interest. Some treat of times, eternal for their stirring events, when the cloud of rebellion was upon the land, and men now famous struggled in the thick darkness. Others trench upon more subdued scenes, having in them much that is ludicrous, while all are seasoned with a "passionate" flavor that cannot fail to tickle the palate of the most sensational epicure.

GEN. H. M. NAGLEE.

In view of the innate love of praise, which is one of the top-gallant passions of the human heart, it is a matter of no small importance for an ordinary man to become, if not celebrated, at least notorious. History furnishes us with many examples of the kind, but fortunately we have an instance near at hand in the person of Henry Morris Naglee. This military gentleman is a native of Philadelphia, which city he honored by his first appearance on the night of January 15, 1815. In 1835, he developed into a full-blown soldier, and graduated at West Point, receiving a commission in an infantry regiment, from which he soon afterward resigned. He then turned civil engineer, which appeared unremunerative, as we find him serving in Lower California during the war with Mexico. He seems to have tired of martial pursuits, as he came to this city (San Francisco) and engaged in mercantile operations, and accumulated a large fortune. From here he went East, and was for a time *employed*

in the army, where, according to the tenor of his let.
ters, he had many miraculous escapes, and did *his
share* towards suppressing the rebellion. From his
own showing, he *was,* if he is not now, a most remarkable man ; and though great as a soldier, he is
still greater in the art of love.

LETTER I.

He hopes she may be happy—Calls her an enchantress—Dreams of her charms—His future wears a brighter hue—Promises to return—and bids his "Little Love good-bye."

SAN JOSE, Dec. 25th, 1858.

MY DEAR LITTLE SWEETHEART:

Merry Christmas! merry Christmas! and may you be truly happy, is my sincere desire; and of this, I hope you will soon feel assured.

What, dear Petite, have been your practices in the necromantic art, for that you have some means of enchantment within your power I am perfectly satisfied—my experience proves it—not only in the extraordinary development of our happy—extremely happy—sympathy of the past, but in the constant spell you have thrown around me, by which I only think and dream of thee. Midst all business, midst all my pleasures, you break through every scene, through every influence. My anticipations, if they be but partly realized, will afford me excessive pleasure, in which you will join. Assure me but of this—assure me but that the sentiment, the feeling, the sympathy is mutual, and I ask no more. Be frank, and I will adore you; but if you conceal anything from me, and do not fully respond to the open, affectionate

11

manner that I have shown towards you, and this with no hesitation and no reserve, I shall be most painfully disappointed, and our sweet anticipation of every pleasure will be turned into deep regret. But no! this cannot be ; you were sincere—your uncertainties, your doubts, have disappeared, and the future, as you assured me already, wears a brighter hue ; you have found one in whom you may place implicit confidence, and who will only love you too well ; whose every care shall be for you, whose every thought shall be to see you happy.

I shall come down on Wednesday, and should you make no other arrangements for our meeting, will come to find you, at three or four o'clock, at your home. Until then, my little love, good-bye—and God bless you, shall be the earnest, sincere wish of

Your

HARRY.

P. S.—I shall look anxiously for that dear little letter you promised me.   H.

LETTER II.

Announces his intense affection—Feels assured that she "dreams
of her Harry"—Dreams a "happy dream" of his "dear
Petite"—Beseeches her to "think of him," and bids adieu
till she "may again whisper in the ear of your dear Harry."

SAN JOSE, January 14th, 1859.

MY DEAR PETITE:

. You will not believe me, my little one ; but I have
thought of you incessantly since ; only night before
last, I saw you and loved you, and felt so really happy
near you. Strange, is it not ? We have only known
each other less than three weeks, and already feel
miserable when separated, though it be for a day. And
yet am I content, for although a little space is between us—although a few hours are necessary to
bring us together—I feel assured that my little sweetheart loves but me—loves, breathes, thinks, dreams,
only of her Harry. I cannot, I would not, think otherwise. I must judge from what I myself feel, and
know that it is but sympathy. It would be worse than
shameful to deceive me—it would be cruel, it would
be wicked.

To me, dear, you have been ever most considerate ;
and, my love, my highest appreciation for you, arises

from a disposition on your part to conform your actions and conduct in such manner as to make me happy, whilst your good judgment has suggested that I would not desire aught that in the end will not lead to your happiness. I dreamed, oh! dear Petite, it was such a dream—such a happy dream—and I slept so well, that all day to-day I have been content. But, love, think now and then of me, and when I return, we will be happy, even in the little relations to each other of all the little incidents that transpired in our absence. So, dear little love, God bless you, good night, adieu, sweet dreams, happy wakings, many contented hours, until you may again whisper in the ear of

Your dear

HARRY.

LETTER III.

Is disappointed at not having heard from his "dear Mary"—
Speaks of her reveries—Promises to return, etc.

SAN JOSE, January 16th, 1859.

MY DEAR MARY:

I am sorely, sorely disappointed, in not receiving one single word from you, but suppose you are completely engrossed in your rehearsals. I had already observed that, on the days of your readings, you were completely exhausted with fatigue, and quite lost in reverie. I would not interfere for the world, and will not return to-morrow, (Monday) as I had intended. I may come down on Wednesday. My kindest recollections to your mother, and am sincerely, affectionately,

Your

HARRY.

LETTER IV.

Is despondent—Fears "his Betsy" does not love him—His nights are sleepless, etc.

San Jose, January 17th, 1859.

My Dear Little Betsy:

Again, another mail, and yet not "one word." Oh! Mary, you cannot, you do not love me.

My nights are sleepless, my days are full of restless anxiety, for I am too truly, devotedly,

Your

Harry.

LETTER V.

Is busily employed—Unable to sleep—Will be disappointed if he does not see his "Dear Betsy"—Believes that he has gone long enough from home, and those that love him, etc.

SAN JOSE, March 25th, 1859.

MY DEAR BETSY:

Since my coming, I have been over-employed. I found everything behind my orders—behind my expectations. I have endeavored to make up for time lost, and have been pressing all work that is behind. I have planted trees; been digging ditches; regulating long lines of troughs; and I can scarcely tell you how much I have been occupied—I know that I get up at half past six every morning, and never return from my place until six at night.

I have to-day commenced fencing, and building a house; and with all this, I have been unable to sleep, and have been quite sick. I shall be down on Sunday. I expect, of course, that you have been at your uncle's, and shall be much disappointed if otherwise.

I have much to tell you, and want very much to see you, indeed. I begin to feel really as though I had been quite long enough from home, and those that love me.

My kindest expressions to Mrs. S——; and am sincerely, truly—too devotedly—your

HARRY.

LETTER VI.

Apologizes for not "calling," and asks her to believe him hers devotedly.

San Francisco, April 12th, 1859.

My Dear Mrs. Schell :

Please don't expect me this evening. I will explain to-morrow, and I know you will forgive me. Give my best respects to your good aunt ; and believe me, sincerely and devotedly, forever, and everywhere,

Your

Harry.

LETTER VII.

Sleeps but little—Soft words to his " dear little sweetheart "—
Will return soon, etc.

SAN JOSE, April 25th, 1859.

MA CHERE PETITE :

No person in the world but yourself, and my promise to you, would or could have induced me to attempt
to write.   I am tired beyond measure ; I slept but little last night, and got up at six this morning.   The
constant exposure in the open country air agrees with
me ; and although tired to death, I am in most excellent health and humor.

Well, my dear little sweetheart, that I love too
much, I only hope you are perfectly well, perfectly
happy, and think occasionally of your homely friend ;
or, rather, as aunt would have said, your homely old
friend.   I shall come on Wednesday, and my first
duty shall be to find my sweet little one.   Adieu, my
dear Mary.

HARRY.

LETTER VIII.

Is miserable—Mourns for his dear Betsy—Philosophizes—Ad-
jures her to be happy—Hopes "Dear Mary" will do nothing to pain "your Harry"—Hot weather—Writes with the
"perspiration rolling off him—Wishes to see Betsy—Sends
her a kiss—Her dear little self is continually before him—
Hopes she will be happy, etc.

STEAMER GOLDEN AGE, }
Saturday, June 11th, 1859. }

MY DEAR, DEAR PETITE :

Five long, weary, fatiguing days, have dragged
themselves along, and I have been most miserable. I
cannot get rid of the extreme depression of spirits
that seems to have complete possession of me. I have
made every effort, but in vain. I can think continually only of my dear little Baby. I only hope she
will have more philosophy ; that she will have courage, and use that better judgment, that strength of
thought, that so ably began to develop itself. Dear
Mary, for your sake, for my sake, for God's sake, pur-
sue the course that lays before you, and you must be,
you shall be happy.

I had much to say to you prior to my coming away,
but your dear little heart was so full, that I could not
allude to my leaving you. But you, dear, dear Mary,

in your own good sense, know all that I would ask of you ; and I feel fully assured you will do nothing that would for one moment pain your Harry.

We have excessively hot weather. I am writing with the perspiration rolling off of me, within a few hours' run of Manzanillo. Mary, I want so much to see you ; and feel and know from my own suffering how very much you suffer. But, dear Mary, I do a sacred duty ; and you, I know, will do and perform the sacred duty that lays before you, and which will make you happy, and make all happy who love and surround you. Dear Mary, I take a sad look at you every day, and send a dear wish and a dear kiss to my Baby. Don't fail to give my kindest remembrances to your mother, and kiss the bird for me. My bible I open every day. And as to your dear little self, if you could but know how continually you are before me, you would be perfectly content. Of your love, dear Mary, I feel assured, and only pray it will lead to your permanent happiness, for that is my only wish, my constant desire. Good-bye, dear, dear Baby. Write to me by every steamer, to Philadelphia.

HARRY.

LETTER IX.

Talks sweet to his "dear little sweetheart"—Begs her to love
him and tell him how long she will be "Harry's exclusive"—Commodore Watkins is kind to the hero—Gives
him coffee after dinner—Is very reserved on the passage—
Crows about his reputation—Hopes his "dear Petite" is
happy—Advises a study of human nature—Has a fit of
logic—Implores her to be herself—Says, to be "happy"
she must "think for herself"—Grows sentimental—Advocates reflection, etc.

STEAMER GOLDEN AGE, NEAR PANAMA, {
17th June, 1859. {

MY DEAR, DEAR BABY:

We will leave this vessel to-morrow morning, and I
am therefore permitted to write to my dear little
sweetheart once more, and feel that she will wait
anxiously to catch every notice of my well-being and
progress. You cannot believe how much I want to
see you, and shall be most anxious until I get your
letter of the 20th of June, and shall be most disappointed if you do not write me everything that
has occurred in detail since my departure. Tell
me how much you love me, and well you love
me, and how long you will be content to be your
Harry's, exclusive of every other thought. Dear
Petite, how does that good old mother of yours

get along? Will she recollect all that I have so often
said to her in regard to your dear self? And I hope
she will do nothing to prevent your carrying out the
good work you have so nobly commenced, and which
I know you will allow nothing to divert you from.

. Commodore Watkins has been exceedingly kind to
me. He placed me on his right at the head of the
table, sends for me every day at one o'clock to lunch
with him, and gives me coffee immediately after dinner in his room, and tea at nine o'clock. He requires
his servant to attend to my wants, and has done all in
his power to make the passage an agreeable one. I
have made very few acquaintances, and have been
even more than usually reserved, which has not
served to detract from my former reputation in that
respect.

Tell me, my dear Petite, are you contented and
happy—do you not feel satisfied that all has been
done for you that could be done to insure your happiness?

My dear little love, you must be a woman. 'Tis
time you should show the strength of your good judgment. Study human nature. Look at the world and
your position in it, not as you would make it, but as it
is. Remember that no one is content—all complain.
How few take advantage of the reasoning judgment
within them; philosophize, and learn to find con-
tentment and happiness in whatever position they
are placed. Dear Mary, you must do this; you must
have a proper ambition, and never let any temporary
pleasure be accepted that will interfere with your permanent welfare. * * * * * *

Be, dear Betsy, my dear Baby, be yourself. But

think, and never determine to act, *except after cool, mature thought.* I would have my little Mary happy, extremely happy, *permanently* contented and happy. I would have her beloved by all of her surrounding friends. And to accomplish this she must think for herself, and act with such good judgment that all will esteem her. But in all of this, dear Betsy, do not, I beg of you, find too much of old reflection. On the contrary, appreciate, as I know you will, and bring up your own sound good .sense, and understand and adopt whatever you may find wholesome, and which you will know is only for your own good. Do you know, my dear Baby, that I never loved you so much as when on one occasion you told me you loved me not so intensely but that you respected yourself the most. Continue, my Betsy, so to do. This proper self-respect is of infinite importance to you, and will lead you to much reflection, and will secure your permanent happiness.

I could write much, and would tire you ; but I must remind you once more of your promises to your Harry ; and after assuring your mother of my kindest regards, * * * I hope you will never fail to believe me, sincerely and devotedly,

Your

HARRY.

LETTER X.

Wants to see Betsy—His mother dies—Suffers from heat and depression—Brags of his reception—His " dearest hope" is to see his Betsy " permanently happy"—Becomes hysterical —Anxiously waits for a "dear letter"—The piano—His hosts of friends—Would be happy if he had his "dear Betsy" near him—Has a gay time in Philadelphia—A bad fit of love, etc.

PHILADELPHIA, July 3d, 1859.

MY DEAR MARY:

How I want to see you! What would I not have given to have you by me. I have, dear Baby, been so very, very sad. I have lost my dear, dear mother. She died the day after I left San Francisco. She counted every hour, every day, every moment, prior to her death, in expectation of my coming. It would have been the greatest possible consolation, could she but have seen her son.

I am suffering from extreme depression, and from the most excessive heat, day and night. It is the same hot, oven-like atmosphere. My immediate relatives and all of my old friends have given me a most hearty, welcome reception. I have been the recipitant of the very warmest evidences of kind esteem, and I assure you, dear Baby, I feel the kindest apprecia-

2

tion of it. I know, my Petite, you will find, next to myself, much satisfaction in all of this, and I shall always be only too happy in adding even ever so slightly to your happiness.

Well, dear sweetheart, are you contented? Does all go on smoothly at your uncle's; for I feel that assurance in your promises that I know you will do anything in the world that your darling Harry desires you should do, especially when you know that his dearest hope is to see you *permanently* happy. Give my kindest remembrances to your mother.

Dear Mary! my dear Baby! my dear, dear Petite! my dear, dear, dear, dear Baby!! I don't love you a bit, and never did, and we never loved each other, and never were happy together.

Don't fail to write to me by every steamer. I am nervously waiting the arrival of the first steamer that shall bring your dear, dear little letter, and wonder what you will tell me. You must tell me all, conceal nothing from me, for your candor and confidence in me has done much for you in gaining my love and esteem. Have you got the piano, and do you practice much? It will be a source of amusement: it will occupy your mind, and serve to remind you of your Harry.

I have scarcely left the house since my arrival. I have been surrounded with my relatives and friends. I have crowds of nephews and nieces, and aunts and cousins, and friends of the family, and friends of my own. My table is covered with invitations, and but for the sad loss of my dear mother, and the absence of my Baby, I could be happy, really happy. I go today to my brother John's, who has a most delightful, beautiful residence at " Chesnut Hill," and shall stay over the Fourth with him. On Tuesday I shall go to * * * and stay a day or two at the residence of my sister Ellen ; on Thursday, to the country residence of my sister Mary ; and thus you see my time is constantly occupied. So, dear Baby, God bless you, and after giving much love to your mother * * * then, dear, darling Baby, retain all of the rest of my love for yourself.

HARRY.

LETTER XI.

Sentiment — Love-sick — Raves — " Hell-fire," " brain," and
" breath"—Wants to see his Betsy happy—Believes in a
" virtuous life"—Reads her letter " every hour of the night"
—A word about Lake—Scents " legal proceedings"—
Promises his love and protection—Desponds—The clock
and little Betsy—Cherishes each word of affection—Becomes loving, etc.

PHILADELPHIA, July 15th, 1859.

MY DEAR, DEAR, BELOVED BABY:

Where shall I begin ?   I have so much to say ; I am
full of feeling, and would give all the world could you
be very near to me, that I might pour out my pent-up
sentiments into your ear.   I want, dear Baby, some
one to hear me talk, and whose every pulsation would
be with mine, who would share my grief and pain with
me, and who would receive my burning tears upon her
dear little heart, and who would respond with her dear
little loving sympathy.   My dear Mary, I think only
of you.   I am possessed night and day of constant
hopes and fears lest you will forget my prayers, and
forget how much I am wrapt up in you.   I would
rather lose every relative there remains to me than
have you go wrong.   I would rather the fires of hell
should enter your brain and breath than that man
should near your lips or touch your hand ; and should

this happen, from thence and forever stop all communication with me. I would never hear your name again. I want, dear Mary, to see you happy; to know that your future shall be a permanently contented, virtuous life.

Your letter, only received last evening, has been read every hour during last night and this morning, and has caused me much pleasure and some pain.

Love, allow no friendships or intimacy from any one whatever, neither Lake or others. You must be exceedingly prudent. If you require counsel, let one of your uncles take that in hand, and let your interview be at your uncle's house, in presence of one of your uncles. But you have necessity for nothing of the kind at present, and during my absence there is necessity for no legal proceedings; and if you have trouble of any kind it must be when I am near you, and will protect and love you. * * * * * *

What, Mary, does the above mean? How unkind, how unlike my dear, confiding, little Petite, who gained so much of the extreme affection I bear her by the unlimited confidence she always placed in me, and this, too, when I am only gone two weeks. I *will not believe* that any other could receive any one word of that confidence that belongs only to me; nor will I believe that you will listen to *one word* from any source whatever that would say aught against your dear darling Harry, or that might be done to disturb your trust and love. Well, I will not scold any longer Before this you will have been convinced that you did me great wrong when you charged me with coolness in my parting with you. My letters—if you love me, and I know it—should console you; should convince you I am not so very, very indifferent. Ar.u what a short little letter you wrote to me ; I was in this disappointed.

How completely, my dear Baby, have you and I, since we were first thrown together on the 23d December—now only six months—completely and e tirely reversed your position. Then you were forsaken by everybody ; now you are beloved by your relations, and intimate confidence restored between you. Then you had no one to care for or protect you ; now your protection is complete, and now, although you may doubt it, you have a darling old Harry, that loves you better than any other living creature. Give my best love to that excellent old mother of yours, and tell her that she must not fail to take care of the two complicated pieces of machinery I have left in her hands ; that the clock will require her attention every Sunday morning, and that the other—my dear, darling little Baby—must receive her constant care. She must love her, or she need not love me ; keep her from all harm, and let her do nothing that would not at once receive the full approbation of her own dear Harry. You see, dear Baby, all the little words of affection you have extended to me are cherished, and are received with pleasure ; and with all this my Baby would be angry, and complain !

Remember me kindly to Aunt Catherine, and say I received her message, " that you are so good a little woman," with extreme satisfaction, and feel too happy in believing that you intend fully to be worthy of her best love and affection. And for yourself all the rest I will keep in reserve, and everywhere and always be your dear, darling, devoted

HARRY.

LETTER XII.

Is melancholy—Is dying to see one little creature—Pictures—
A love fit—1 ___ of his ugliness—Becomes homesick—
Sheds tears, etc.

PHILADELPHIA, July 17th, 1859.

MY DEAR BABY:

I forgot to ask you for the address of your aunt
and grandmother, that if you desire it, I may go and
see them. Petite, I am very, very sad; I find but
little to amuse me. I have every reason to be contented with the exceeding kindness of my relations
and friends; but I find little or no gratification in
meeting so many. There is one little creature only
that I am dying to see; and with her, and near her,
my thoughts are constantly clinging.

I have two pictures constantly near me : one in an
oval case of red velvet, and it represents a lady of
about twenty; the expression is of sadness and thought,
as though she thought intensely of one that was very
dear to her, but who might be absent from her. The
other is of a lady of the same age, in ordinary framed
case; but she has a sweet smile, as though she felt
secure and certain of the devotion of him who has so
often given her assurances and evidences of his affection. Dear Baby, be my guardian dream; let me

think and believe that I control your star; and the *motive* and my *object* is so *pure*, that to me it is a source of immense satisfaction.

I have been trying to recollect what act of mine, prior to my leaving, appeared to you one of coldness, and can recall only that of not leaving a daguerreotype. Why should you desire to have near you so ugly and old gray head? Your dear little imagination, I know, keeps before you a much more comely one, and the comparison is thus much in my favor. However, I will surprise you and send you one, but let it be kept in your sanctum, and shown to no one.

Oh, my dear, dear Baby! how exceedingly sad I am; the tears will course down my cheeks. I have no satisfaction in remaining in my old home; it is now one of pain and sadness. Every shrub and flower, every room, every little piece of furniture, everything animate and inanimate, has now for me only the most melancholy association, and I am compelled to look elsewhere to pass my dreary hours. Oh, my dear, dear Baby! how dearly did my dear, dear mother love her absent son. We should have closed her eyes, and she would have died so happily, and I should be so very, very much more content. I can write no more.

Your dearly devoted

HARRY.

LETTER XIII.

is happy—Receives a letter from Betsy—Desires to rest his
" burning brow " upon her " dear bosom "—Enthusiasm—
Advocates employment—Suspicions—Lake—Speaks of
portraits—Wants to emigrate—Kisses—Moralizes, etc.

New York, August 1st, 1859.

My Dear, Dear Baby :

You will never know how extremely happy your
dear, loving letter made me.   It was a solace to my
troubled heart ; it was a soothing balm to my wearied
spirit.   I have been, my dear, dear Petite, so very unhappy ; and I have no one near me upon whose
bosom I would lean and give vent to my excessive
agony.   Oh, dear, dear Mary ! what a great relief it
would be, if I could but rest my burning brow upon thy
dear bosom, and tell thee all I feel, and receive thy
dear consoling sympathy in return.   I know my tears
would be thy tears, and thy tears would be a sweet,
dear consolation and support.   But, dear Baby, this
is not proper, to worry you unnecessarily ; you have
had quite enough trouble of your own, without any
portion of mine on your dear little self.   Oh, how much
satisfaction I feel that your * * has received you
back near his heart.   This gives me another and a very
great assurance that your future will be one of much

happiness ; that soon all memory of the pains of the past will be forgotten, and my dear Betsy will assume that position among her many warm friends that she is entitled to. My dear Love, let me ask you to have some employment always near you. You can sew ; you can knit ; you can practice your piano—do anything ; but do not find yourself idle. And my dear Baby did her darling Harry great injustice ; and, bless her dear little soul, her dear little heart reproved her, and she, with all her truthfulness and justice, acknowledged the wrong she had done her dear Harry.

Dear Baby, take no notice of anything you may hear of me in San Francisco. They will deceive you, to undermine the affection you have for me. Any one who will say aught to you of me, rely upon it, is no friend of yours or mine. Fear nothing, but rely on me, and your own cool judgment. Any person who will speak in any unfriendly manner of me, stop him, and change the subject, or leave the room.

Dear Baby, I expect your next letter will tell me that my requests with regard to Lake are properly heeded, and that I may rest satisfied on that subject. I am very angry that William should have annoyed you. I have directed that he should be discharged from my employment.

I commenced this letter three days gone by, and I am constantly interrupted ; but I hope to make out sufficiently for my dear little Sweetheart, to convince her she is always nearest my thoughts, and nearest to my heart.

I send you my picture, that I did not promise to send ; but you must receive it on two conditions : first, I would suggest that, under all circumstances, it is as

well to take down from a prominent position at your
mother's, the picture of *   * ; and, second, that
you promise me you will show my picture to no person whatever, but keep it entirely *to* and for *yourself;*
you may look when you please, as I do, constantly, on
the two I have, but no one else ; mine are sacred, and
go with me wherever I go. You see, Love, how much
of Christian goodness I can advise ; and when near
you, or when my thoughts are engaged in your welfare, it has always been thus.

Write me much about your mother, I like to hear
of her and from her. I shall answer her very kind
letter.

I cannot stay in my old home, it is dreadfully sad
to me. I do not like Philadelphia. I am already
tired of New York, and think of going into the wine
districts of France. I hope you have been to see my
place, and expect a detailed account of your visit.
The kind notice of my leaving, which you sent to me,
was the more satisfactory because I know it gratified
my dear Petite, and to her I know a source of pride
that I should so signally triumph over those that
would do evil.

Dear Baby ! Dear Mary ! Dear Petite ! and Dear
Betsy ! I kiss you all, with a kiss that you know is
sincere, that you know comes from the depths of my
heart and soul, and which you know it would be rank
injustice to doubt for an instant. I have just read
your letter for the five hundredth time ; I believe I
have fully answered every suggestion you have made,
and so, dear, dear Love, God bless you ; as I love
you, be a good, a very good and excellent woman, and
let every bodylove you but the one-hundredth part as

I love you, and you will be worshiped ; but in all of this be deserving of yourself, and of the esteem of all others ; be thoughtful, and let your cool and better judgment always prevail, and when *you* doubt, I want you to advise with no one, but rely on yourself; then if there be a doubt do as you say you do in your sweet little letter : " *To act as your Dear Harry would have you act.*"

My love to your good mother; so once more, with all my thoughts, and dreams, and prayers, I am devotedly your

HARRY.

LETTER XIV.

Out of humor—Love-sick—Tombstones—Henry E. Robinson—Coughs—Love-letters—Robinson again—the "dear little Sweetheart."

PHILADELPHIA, August 22d, 1859.

MY DEAR, DEAR PETITE:

Your dear little favor of the 2d of July was not received until three or four days after the steamer's letters came in, and then it came by the overland coach; in good time, however, to relieve me of much ill-humor, which was venting itself upon all of the post offices and Postmasters between this and San Francisco. I never for one moment believed you had not written, but, on the contrary, was as fully certain of it, as if your letter had been already before me. Many kind thanks, Dear, Dear Baby, to yourself and mother, for your kind sympathy; I know precisely where I shall find an echo to my sad misfortune; I know the dear little heart that would respond in one sympathetic throb with my distress, and that your tears would flow after mine in bitter anguish. I have been engaged for the last two weeks in preparing plans and in selecting a location for a tomb for my mother's and father's remains; my mother, in her last hours, desired that her body might lay near his, and this is my present duty, to carry out this with other requests she desired might be left for her dear, dear Henry to execute. Oh! dear Mary, why did you not send me away sooner from San Francisco, that I might have closed my mother's eyes in peace and happiness. My absence was the only thing that distressed her in her dying. Had she only been allowed to have embraced her dear son she would have died perfectly happy. She was beloved everywhere; she was known by all that were in want of a protector; she was the friend to all the poor little children of her neighborhood, and her name is a household word of simple goodness. Indeed, I have lost the best friend I ever had; hers was for me truly a mother's love; intense, devoted.

SUNDAY, Sept. 4th.

The steamer sails to-morrow, and I must finish this little note, commenced a week ago. I have been here in New York since Tuesday last. I have been near my friend Henry E. Robinson, who is quite sick; he is having an operation performed upon his throat by Dr. Green, for a bronchial affection from which he has suffered for the last eight years. I am watching the progress of his cure with much interest, for if successful I will endeavor to have mine cured, for you may recollect I have suffered from an irritation and cough from a like cause for a year or more. For the last two or three days I have felt quite unwell, I have a headache and much depression, and to-day I feel so unwell I would prefer to go to bed, and will do so as soon as I finish my letters. I have as yet received no letter by the last steamer, and suppose you sent your letter as before by the overland coach. This would do very well for an intermediate letter, but for letters of the steamer day there is a difference in favor of the steamer to New York of at least three days. However, my dear Mary, I will not complain if you will only write, for to me it is a vast satisfaction to receive your dear little loving letters. I am very sorry to learn that your mother suffers from rheumatism, especially as it may require her to give up our house in which she has been so comfortable, and in which so much was accomplished for my dear Petite. Mr. Robinson is an old and confidential friend—I shall give him a letter to you, he is of Sacramento. I hope, my dear Mary, you continue to carry out all of the good resolutions you formed, and I know the result will be most happy, most satisfactory to yourself, to myself, and to all of your many friends. Dear, dear little sweetheart, I want you to give my love to your mother, much kind respect to your uncle and his family, and retain all the rest for your own dear, dear self.

HARRY.

LETTER XV.

A letter—Judge Field and * * * cottage—Mr. and Mrs. *
John Perry — Wants a thousand details — Fifth Avenue
Hotel—Love in a cot—Robinson—A storm—Leases his
theater to Baker—Tom Maguire—Mr. Sime—Love talk—
Logic—Advises Betsy to be a ' good girl "—Implores her
to write, etc.

FIFTH AVENUE HOTEL, New York, }
September 19th, 1859. }

MY DEAR, DEAR PETITE :

Your letter of the 19th of August was duly received,
following one of 21st of July, by the overland mail ;
none as yet of the beginning of August, which must
have miscarried.   I am here for, the purpose of seeing
my friends Judge Field and lady, and shall return
to Philadelphia immediately after the departure of the
steamer.   I have been quite unwell for the last two
weeks, but feel for a day or two a little better.   I
think, dear Mary, you will like the cottage on Green
street.   The location is a good one, with views very
beautiful all around you, and there you will be near
my friend Mrs. Perry and Mr. John Perry, that I
have desired so much you should know.   I am sure
you will love Mrs. Perry, she is so very good, and kind,
and amiable.   My dear Baby, you do not tell me how
you pass your time ; you do not enter into any of the

detail of your occupations ; you might tell me a thousand things, but you don't choose to do so.

This hotel is really beautiful, but most miserably managed. I am in the top story—as near heaven as I ever was, and cannot get nearer to the earth. I shall leave it this afternoon—it is too high a distinction for me, and I won't endure it ; you know my tastes are of a different order—love in a cottage, in a brown house, anywhere ; but the sixth story of the Fifth Avenue Hotel, without that requisite, and I am displeased—very much annoyed. My friend Robinson does not go out by this steamer, and I must defer sending you what I promised you until I can do so by him, which will certainly be by the next.

A dreadful storm swept over the entire country for the last three days, and trees, and houses, and people, and everything and everybody, suffered. I learn that my theater is leased to Baker. This I do not altogether like ; I should have preferred to have left him with his friend Tom Maguire. But I suppose, of course, Mr. Sime did the best he knew how, and I can ask no more of him. Well, dear, dear Baby, I have not, in all my sojourn on this side for three months, enjoyed as much pleasure and real happiness as I always did in any one evening with my dear, dear Betsy ; so it is, we never know the future, we never know when we are well off. I hope your mother has completely recovered her health, and that she will continue to occupy the brown house. I am so happy to know you are in such excellent relations with your uncle. * * * The only wonder I have is, that midst so many to do you homage, you are not completely spoiled. I always thought you more than half spoiled before my influences were brought to bear upon you, but I must say, after you began to love me, you improved very rapidly ; you are now *beginning* to be of mature, ripened, experienced age ; you have of late had the use of your thinking powers, and I am sure ought to be able to arrive at very proper conclusions on all important subjects. Lord, dear Mary, how much I have to talk to you about; how many questions I could propose ; what a book you have to read to me, and then what a sweet chapter we would just peruse on our joint account. Give my love to your mother, be a good, dear Betsy, and never fret nor worry, nor be unhappy unnecessarily ; be my dear, sweet, confiding, brave, courageous, thoughtful Petite ; be *yourself* as I know you—*strong, determined,* VIRTUOUS, and *enduring*—and of all things, don't fail to write every time a steamer leaves. You should appreciate my happiness in receiving your letters by yours in receiving mine, and my disappointment is great when I fail to do so. God bless you forever.

HARRY.

LETTER XVI.

Bilious fever—A Picture — " A swell " — "Dear Betsy, scold away "—Mrs. Perry—Caresses—Robinson — Cars — Love and respect—God bless you, etc.

PHILADELPHIA, October 4th, 1859.

MY DEAR PETITE:

Your darling letter of September 4th was received, with, at the same time, one from your mother, and a package from your * * *. I had been sick for a week with the bilious fever in New York, and did not return until day before yesterday. Your uncle's business is of that importance to him, that I shall return to New York this afternoon and endeavor to determine it prior to the sailing of the steamer to-morrow. We have had the most disagreeable equinoctial weather, and I found myself completely laid up. I, however, submitted to a good purging, and feel much relieved. Well, my dear Baby, you found your picture quite like the original. I am sorry it has not the latest style of his dress—the *choke* neck collar and " *tie*." You have no idea how much my appearance is altered thereby; indeed, to that extent, that a few days since I was going up Chesnut street, when some five or six boys were coming along with a wheelbarrow, and one turned round to the rest and told them to "stop the wheelbarrow and let that dandy pass." I blushed, was much confused, thanked the boys for their extreme consideration and politeness, and passed on. What a very little humbug you are; and you want to scold me, do you? Well, I can only say, dear Baby, scold away; I will take it all peaceably from you; I assure you I won't get angry at anything my spoiled Baby may say. I am most happy to hear that your mother is quite well.

Well, my dear little Love, have you moved to the new house—have you made the acquaintance of Mrs. Perry? How do you do—how do you look? Are you as little, as dear a little Baby as I always loved to caress so closely? I hope, Mary, you will find occupation always. I desire that you should do so; it will add much to your happiness, and I know you will do so. My friend Robinson is still very ill, and is under the care of Dr. Green; he is unable to leave for California; he has suffered very much from his throat and nose. I have but one hour left to eat my dinner and get to the cars for New York; so, my dear, dear Baby, after taking all of the affection and love you want for yourself, turn over a little to your mother. God bless you, my dear, dear Betsy.

Affectionately,

HARRY.

LETTER XVII.

Business—Europe—Desires to be near Betsy—New ideas—
Asks advice—Sentiment—Sick brother, etc.

PHILADELPHIA, October 19th, 1859.

MA CHERE PETITE:

Your dear little letter of the 19th ulto. is before me, and has been faithfully devoured. I went to New York after receiving the letter of your * * *, and was much disappointed in not being able to conclude the business intrusted to me. However, I did the best I knew, and left it as he had instructed me to leave it.

The cold weather is commencing, and I think seriously of making a trip to Europe. I have never been better prepared to do so, and I fear if I do not take advantage of my present position, I shall never have another as favorable. Baby, what do you think of it— I mean as a dear little friend, a disinterested adviser, who was asked her cool, deliberate, friendly counsel? I don't know whether you can fairly give your dispassionate opinion upon the subject; you can hardly divest yourself of certain old sentiments which might influence you in your decision. Well, my dear, dear Baby, I would be exceedingly happy to balloon myself, and drop very, very close to you, and there remain in one sweet, soft embrace for one whole month. Do you think you would get tired of me? Do you think you could then be persuaded to send me off to Europe? Don't you think, my dear Betsy, I ought to go? Don't you think it would give me many new ideas?—leave me much to think of, much to talk to you about? I could be so happy in relating to you all I had seen, and all I had heard. This would be worth all the pain and sacrifice attending our separation.

My brother is very sick with a typhoid fever; he is at his country residence, some ten miles in the country. I am going within an hour to see him, and shall remain until he gets better.

Give my love to Mrs. Sheppard, and much respect to all my friends, and to you, my dear, dear, devoted Baby, all the rest.

HARRY.

LETTER XVIII.

A letter—Josh Haven and Charles Brenham—Mr. Janes—
Business—Paul Morphy—Chess—Paintings — Reflections
on Betsy—Mrs. Samuel Hermann—Advises system—Loving, as usual, etc.

PHILADELPHIA, November 4, 1859.

MY CHERE, CHERE PETITE:

Your dear little letter of October 4 was duly received, and fully and entirely consumed ; every word,
every line, every thought and every feeling, therein in-
dicated is, I assure you, my dear, dear Baby, fully
responded to.

You saw, you say, Josh Haven and Charles Brenham in my box, and therefore *suppose* they are friends
of mine. Oh ! you saucy little creature. What do you
mean ? What saucy idea have you concealed under
this ? Baby, I left my box in charge of my attorney
and agent, Mr. Janes, and any persons who occupy it
do so, I suppose, by his invitation or consent. I am
so happy your mamma is so much better, and only hope
she may never be more unhappy than when seeing the
elephant with Robby.

Your Uncle * * *'s affairs I have placed, as he directed, in charge of his attorney in New York, and
suppose, of course, he is fully informed by him of

everything he has done. I regret very much there should have been any difficulty about them.

Well, my dear, dear Baby, I have been entertaining myself very much in showing some civility to Paul Morphy, the great American chess player, and am very much pleased with him. He is, as you know, just of age. His appearance is very youthful ; his stature exceedingly small. He is very retiring in his manner, very modest in his conduct. His position is vastly superior, by the reputation he has made, to that of any young man in the world. I have lately been to see some very fine pictures, and sat long, and take great pleasure in looking at them. And then I like to be alone. I like to lie in bed and muse, and let my mind wander. I am much relieved that I never recur to any business. I never think of the troublesome affairs I had in San Francisco. But I do think, dear, dear Baby, very often of thee and thine, and I do console myself that your mind is rapidly maturing, and you will soon be of that sound judgment that smaller matters will no longer trouble you, and that learning much of this bad old world, you will expect less from it, and find less disappointment. Be, my Baby, very calm ; always take a night to reflect on anything important; be a dear little philosopher.

It is eleven o'clock, and Mr. Morphy and Mr. Tricou, son of Mrs. Sam Herman, have just come into my room to advise me they are ready for breakfast ; so my Petite Betsy, my dear, dear Betsy, be of good cheer for your own account, for my account, that it will make you more happy, that it will add much to mine. Be systematic in everything. Have an hour for everything—an hour to rise, an hour to breakfast.

an hour to read, an hour to dress, an hour to walk, and an hour to work ; an hour to write, for you would find it amusing to keep every day a little memorandum of the important occurrences that might be worth remembering ; and then it makes a variety in your daily occupations. My love to your mamma, and to all of those who love you. For your own dear, dear little self, I am everywhere and always your dearly devoted

HARRY.

LETTER XIX.

Chat—Complains of Betsy—Philosophy—Plunges into dissipation—Picture of his mother—Implores Betsy to be
happy.

PHILADELPHIA, November 17, 1859.

MY DEAR PETITE:

Your dear little missive of October came to me
only yesterday ; and inasmuch as I am compelled 'o
go to Washington to-morrow, and fearing that something might deter me from writing, I will take time by
the forelock, and write in advance of the mail.   And
so you have moved on to Green street.   I hope you
have made the acquaintance of my friends Mr. and
Mrs. Perry, and that you and the latter will become
very good friends.   I am much indebted for your very
kind, friendly interest in my affairs at San José, and I
shall not fail to inquire into all you suggest.   I have
done all I can do in your Uncle * * * 's business, and
have written to him on the subject.   I have not heard
lately from his attorney.

Why, what a cross little Baby my Betsy will determine to be.   She will complain, in spite of all and
everything that everybody tries to do for her ; and it
seems to me she should endeavor to be more like the
rest of the world, and be more content.   We cannot

have everything just as we would like to have it ; nobody ever did, or nobody ever will ; and you need not expect to be the exception. Why have you not long since discovered that to grumble is man's prerogative, his great privilege, without which man would be miserable indeed. I never knew man, woman, or child that did not find excessive pleasure in grumbling, and therefore I do not find it strange in thee.

Well, dear love, I have been passing some weeks more agreeably. I have had some friends under my especial charge, and have been plunged into much dissipation ; not such as you, with all the affectionate care you would throw around me, would criticise too closely. I have been *fêted* until I dine out four or five times every week, and am invited to evening parties nearly every night, and scarcely ever get to bed until 2 A.M. I stand it better than I could have hoped, but I have become prudent, and take great care of myself.

I have had a picture painted of my mother, and the artist has succeeded very well. The picture gives great satisfaction to the family. Give much love to your good mother ; and I am happy that she is well, and contented in her cottage. And, dear Baby, be happy ; do try to find some employment that is agreeable. Do as I have so often suggested, and advise me of the effect. The letter of August never came to me ; so you owe me one. I am quite well, and love devotedly my dear Betsy.

HARRY.

LETTER XX.

Washington—Army friends—Harry grows stout—Becomes
"rigid in his hours"—Tires of dissipation—Gymnastic
exercises—Bath-tub—Love—Harper's Ferry—Politics—
Brother Billings—Longs to be near Betsy—His style of living—Adams & Co.—"Oceans of pleasure"—The "old
sofa"—A fierce love fit, etc.

WASHINGTON, D. C., Dec. 1st, 1859.

MA CHERE PETITE:

I have been here for the last two weeks, in connec-
tion with some business of importance for some particular friends at San José. The "Baltic" arrived in
New York the 27th of November, but the mail has
not yet arrived. It generally comes in four or five
days after the other line. Your mails must arrive
with the same irregularity. I am compelled to write
before I get your letter, for fear I shall not get it
until too late for the steamer of the fifth, and I will
not risk the probabilities of loss from Philadelphia.
I have passed my time very agreeably here. I have
seen many old army friends, and have been looking
at the vast improvements in the public buildings. I
shall return to Philadelphia next week. The weather
has been delightful—no cold winter as yet; on the
contrary, the last two weeks have been almost Califor-

nian. I suppose you are pleasantly settled down in
your new home, more pleasantly located by far than
that on Powell street, although farther off from the
cottage—and Robby.

Well, dear Baby, you would hardly know your
Harry, he has grown so stout. I have, through necessity, become very rigid in my hours. I found I
could not stand so much entertainment, and being up
until one and two o'clock A.M. every night, was too
much of a good thing. I take gymnastic exercises
every morning in my bath-tub, and this has added
much to my health.

PEN AND INK SKETCH AS DRAWN BY HIMSELF

Don't you see, Betsy, how it is done. I raise myself from this—I mean the above position—until my arms are straight, and let myself down. I commenced with doing this half a dozen times, and could do no more; now I do so twenty times. I do so every morning. My arms are double the size they were a month ago. I would just like to see you try it—not in your tub, for that is too small. I had not discovered, when I recommended that tub so strongly, the grand combination tub, uniting the gymnastic exercises with bathing. The inventive genius of the Yankee nation is truly astonishing and unlimited. I see by the papers the steamer with the mails has arrived, and I will not have an opportunity of reading your dear little letter for two or three days. I know it will bear keeping that long.

There has been an immense excitement all over the country caused by the Harper's Ferry affair. The feeling between the Abolitionists and Slave-owners is at fever heat; and the alarms throughout the South, lest there should be an insurrection, are constant and ridiculous. Nine-tenths of the Northern people are against the fanatics, and they would not permit any attempt at any negro insurrection; besides, it has been demonstrated in the late Harper's Ferry affair that the negroes won't go against their masters. In that, the negroes were the only ones who behaved well throughout; and certainly they deserve much credit, not only for their conduct then, but ever since. Indeed, I have no hesitation in believing the negroes could have been safely armed to oppose the Abolitionists. However, you take no interest in all of this, and only care to be let alone. What a selfish little creature is our Betsy! She is the veriest little despot living, and will only issue her edicts, and expect all to obey.

How does the church get along, and Brother Billlings, and the subscriptions; and is my dear little Baby growing taller, or wider, or more good, or more wise, or more saucy? Does she look like her pretty little sad face, that I look at so often, or has she become more matronly? Does Aunty Shephard still patronize all the vendors of good things that come along? You see I am very curious. I have ten thousand questions to ask, and were I near you, I should have more than you could answer for a month; indeed, there would be but one way, and that would be to shut yourself up with me, and let me propound and you answer.

Well, dear, dear Betsy, I have got my time so regulated that I can hardly tell you how rapidly it passes. I get up at nine, am bathed and dressed, shaved and shirted by ten; I breakfast by eleven; visit from half past twelve to half past two; take a nap at half past three; dine at six; visit from eight to ten, or if there be a reunion, it lasts until one. Thus the time flies, and I am recovering my better spirits. I am forgetting the cross, ill nature engendered in me by Adams & Co., and other like subjects that harassed me so much and so long. My friends hardly recognize in me the same person. My feelings and looks are really changed. If there be anything in your letter that I have not anticipated, I will write by overland mail. It is reported here, and I am afraid only with too much truth, that Vanderbilt has purchased out the Atlantic and Pacific Companies, and that he is the sole owner of all the lines between California and this country. This is bad news for our side.

Well, my darling little pet, be of good cheer; I shall have volumes to tell you when I get back; and in that will I have oceans of pleasure. Indeed, we will wear out the old sofa, for we will not care to sit anywhere else. How I wish I was just there now, and had you just as near to me as you would like to be. Oh, Betsy! would we not be just the happiest, sauciest, lovingest little pair ever known. God bless you, dear Betsy, be a darling, sweet little Baby, and believe your Harry loves you too well, too dearly.

HARRY.

My love to your mother, of course.

LETTER XXI.

Christmas—Romps—Insurance—" Ugly as Satan "—Judge
Hoffman — Poulterer — San Jose — Affectionate remarks,
etc.

PHILADELPHIA, Dec. 25, 1859.

MY DEAR, DEAR BETSY :

A very happy Christmas to you, and may they return every year finding you more happy than that
which preceded it. Oh ! how cold it is to-day ; the
streets are filled with ice, and few people to venture outside their houses. I thought I should freeze last
night, it was intensely cold ; to-day I did not get up
until ten o'clock, and at one I went to see my brothers
and sisters and all of their children. I have had a
good romp. I am much disappointed in not receiving
any letters from you. Your uncle * *'s business is still at
a stand ; the additional affidavits have been received. I
was compelled to look up the original protest about a
week ago. That was sent to this city. The Insurance
Co. are behaving badly, and ought to be exposed in
your papers.

I am enjoying myself in a very quiet way, and am
nearly all the time within doors, for it is really too
cold to go out. I returned from Washington, and

have been here since. I am told everything looks
well with you, and that you have abundance of rain.
Well, Baby, time runs on and I have done nothing
since, here, but rest my overwrought brain, and no one
knows better than your dear little self how necessary
it was for me. I expect to return feeling much
younger than when I came away, although as ugly as
ever ; and in that you will be pleased, for you always
wished I would become as ugly as Satan. I saw
Judge Hoffman, Poulterer and wife, and some others.
You never sent me the address of your grandmother
and aunt in New York, I should have liked to have
called and seen them ; I know my visit would have
given them much satisfaction, for I could have said
much about my dear little Baby that would have
pleased them. I keep up the gymnastics, and have
increased the duration of the exercise considerably ; I
find myself, in consequence of it, much improved in
strength.

I am much obliged for the pigeons, and will send
you some of the squabs. I have written inquiring
particularly about my affairs in San Jose from some
friends. I learn that, generally speaking, my place
looks well, that the grapes and trees nearly all took
root, although they suffered much from the gophers.
Robert writes that he has killed nearly all the squirrels,
and as many as 350 gophers. Thank God, the ex-
pense of construction is nearly finished, it has been
so much more than I thought it could be ; do you
recollect how my Baby used to be annoyed when I
went to San Jose, and how she would pout and scold
when I stayed longer than anticipated ? Why, Baby,
what would have become of me but for the relief ob-

tained through my place? Don't you know the old
proverb, "that too much work," &c., &c. ; well, I
am making my letter so long that you won't read it,
and so with love to your mother and others, and all
the rest for my dear, dear Betsy, I am sincerely and
devotedly her own darling

HARRY.

LETTER XXII.

Mrs. Perry—Loves the pictures—Moralizes on matters of
the heart—Cold—Baths and gymnastic exercises—
Sweet-talk about the "little baby woman"—Overland
Mail—Hopes for the "long letter"—"Ten thousand long
sweet kisses."

PHILADELPHIA, Jan. 19, 1860.

MY OWN DEAR PETITE:

The only letter received from you for a long time
bears date 8th of December, and this I received yesterday. I had been absent for three weeks in the interior of the State, and only returned yesterday. It
has been intensely cold, and I have suffered severely;
I cannot keep my feet warm. I am very happy to
learn you have made the acquaintance of Mrs. Perry,
and am more happy to know that you confirm all I
ever said to you in her favor. I know you will love
her the more the longer you know her; you want to
know if I ever see my pictures—for don't forget that
I have two—certainly I see them, always; I hardly
know which to love the most, the one that smiles or
the one that looks sad; but this depends much upon
my own humor, for in all of these matters of the
heart all is a matter of sympathy, and I love it, for

without true feeling sympathy there is no real love. I regret very much to hear of your aunt's sickness, but know that it was an excellent opportunity to have shown her how much you love her.

Oh ! dear Betsy, this wretchedly cold weather makes a Californian love his country. I would not exchange one year of Californian living, so far as the weather is concerned, for a dozen of such as this they suffer in the North. I passed Christmas and New Year's days with my relatives, in a very quiet, domestic way, much to their satisfaction and much to that of the children and to mine. I have become quite a hermit, and remain much in the house. I don't like the cold and I don't like the house ; these coal fires and constant confinement don't agree with me, and but for my bath and gymnastic exercises I could not stand it, but I keep them up very regularly.

Well, love, how do you do ? are you a dear, sweet, mild, amiable little baby-woman as you tried to be for your darling Harry ; or are you a restless, ungovernable, strange little creature without reason ? but I know you cannot deceive me, you don't like your Harry to be away ; but you recollect what he told you, and your second thoughts always advise you well ; don't they, my Baby, you little, naughty creature ; you will occasionally let a little ill-humor slip, and your second thoughts remind you of it, and you correct yourself ; is it not well that I understand you so very well ? I will write again soon.

The letters by overland mail require twenty-seven to twenty-eight days, but I believe the mail by Vanderbilt's steamers requires as much. I am anxiously awaiting your " *long letter you intend to write by the steamer*"

It has not yet arrived ; my love to your good mother
and to everybody at your aunt's ; and to yourself all
the rest, with ten thousand long, sweet kisses.

Your own

HARRY.

LETTER XXIII.

On the "wing"—A family difficulty—The cold subjugates the "war horse"—He is anxious about the "old sofa"—Desires to return to California — Apostrophizes his "little Petite"—Avows his love, etc.

STEAMER CANADA, NEAR HALIFAX, ⎱
February 23d, 1860. ⎰

MY BELOVED PETITE:

Your favor of the 19th of January was received, as I informed you, and I expected, when I wrote to you, to see your aunt and grandmother; but, in consequence of a heavy snow-storm, I was detained on the road between Philadelphia and New York thirteen hours—nine hours more than the usual time—and by the time I had got through with my business, preparatory to my voyage, I found it impossible to get through with much important business, and the visit to your relatives. I regret this, dear, because I expected to have made you happy in relating all that would have passed.

I am very sorry, love; indeed, I am. Dear Baby, I wrote to you in reply to that portion of your letter referring to the indiscretion of your * * *, and am sorry that you did not use your better judgment; you should have visited Mrs. P. as usual, and waited some good occasion when you could well have made an easy explanation. Under any circumstances, be not annoyed ; fortunately, it is of that kind of report so very common, that they are heard, and repeated, and forgotten, and generally without any explanation. I don't see that either *you* or *I* can suffer any in consequence of it, and, therefore, fret no more. My love to your good mother ; say I am going across the Atlantic, but that this convinces you that the next direction will be for *our* home. I would not stay another winter on this side for anything ; it is as much as one's life is worth.

Dear love, send your letters as heretofore ; my agent is instructed to forward them to me. Well, Betsy, take care of that old sofa, for I shall want some comfortable place to rest after I return, and there was none where I was made so happy as on that sofa, and in that cottage. I wrote to your Uncle Robert, but, of course, I can do nothing to forward his interests ; I have done all that I could do. I shall write on my arrival in England, and it will be some twenty-three or more days after the date of this before you can receive it. Be brave, love ; have proper resolution ; it cannot be long before I return. I am getting very tired of everything away from San Francisco, and I can assure you I am very anxious to get back—the weather, the people, your letters, all make me want to return.

Dear Petite, your sweet, loving confidence in your Harry is fully appreciated ; you cannot be driven from him, he has stood by you through many and all difficulties, and he is proud to know that he has never been mistaken in his little Petite ; and he feels per-

fectly satisfied that she has now that strength of judgment and that determination, that she is safe from all
harm, and from all the evil purposes of the too many
evilly disposed. Continue, love, to be the same, and
rely on him who loves you dearly, devotedly, and who
holds your only love and sympathy.

LETTER XXIV.

In London—The "war horse" sees the elephant—Sighs for his
"darling Petite," etc.

LONDON, March 14th, 1860.

MY OWN DARLING PETITE:

Here am I, completely lost, feeling as much alone
as though upon a deserted island. I keep myself
employed in seeing the many things I have so often
heard and read of before. I went to the West-
minster Abbey, and saw the tombs of royalty and
merit all crumbling to dust together.

I saw the houses of Parliament, the Crystal Palace,
the Regent, Hyde and St. James parks, all beautiful
in the extreme. I went to the West End and to the
Zoological Gardens. I went into Covent Garden, and
heard a new opera, Lurline. I went to the old Hay-
market, and Drury Lane, and Olympic, and to the
El Dorado and Argyll entertainments; then I went to
Canterbury Hall, and into the famous gin and beer
palaces. Thus, you see, dear Betsy, I have been
going—going—going; and with all, dear Petite, I am
sad. I want much to see you. I would give worlds
to see you—to have you here, that you might go with
me, and see with me, and feel with me the influences

of these mighty structures ; they are, many of them, immense. Old St. Paul looks gray with age and smoke, and towers over everything in the clouds. Victoria Tower is beautiful in the extreme, and the pictures in the National Gallery should occupy a month. My love to your mother ; write as heretofore ; my agent will forward your letters to me. So, dear little love, with a feeling God bless you, I am truly and sincerely

Your

HARRY.

LETTER XXV.

The " war horse" in Paris—He talks like a Stoic—London and Paris—French and English women—Rare sights—Mrs. P——y—Spain—Likes her letters—Moralizes—Loves her —Homesick, etc.

HOTEL AU LOUVRE, PARIS,
April 8, 1860.

MA CHERE PETITE:

Your dear, sweet, saucy, little notes of February 6th and 20th were received only day before yesterday, and am most happy to find, in spite of the usual number of complaints, that you are quite well. How have you succeeded in convincing yourself that you are the most miserably abused person in the world? Why, Betsy, you should receive the condoling sympathy of all kind hearted people. You should be the concentration of the prayers of the righteous that you should be able to find no annoying subject to dwell upon. Well, Baby, here am I, in this wonderful city, among these wonderful Parisiennes. I have seen something of the city, but have much, very much to see. I liked England, but not London. I like Paris, but not France. The country in the interior of England is perfectly beautiful. The City of London is smoky and black,

and gloomy. The interior of France that I have seen
was not at all inviting. The City of Paris is magnifi-
cent, brilliant, filled with everything beautiful and entertaining. The women in London were of beautiful,
clear, fair complexions, rather gross and awkward,
with large feet and hands. The women of Paris are
ugly, but are perfectly familiar with all of the arts of
embellishing and beautifying. They take every advantage of dress, and are very cleanly. They all are
very polite. You find the shops filled with thousands
of pretty things ; and the restaurants do know how to
produce the most exquisite nice dishes ; and good
wine is most abundant. You see, then, some of the
reasons why a man may pass a few days pleasantly
in Paris.

I am sorry you have avoided Mrs. P——y ; it was
childish ; it was very very wrong on your part. Go
and see her at once. You will find her, as I have always told you, amiable, and reasonable, and just.
She will kiss you, and ask you to forgive and forget,
and that in all probability was her desire in coming to
find you. Oh, Petite, what a strange little creature ;
you have not the strength I had always given you
credit for. Courage, ma chere Petite.

I go from Paris to-morrow, and will be in Spain
within a few days.

Write as heretofore. All of your letters will come
to me ; and although they come long after they are
written, they are not less appreciated. They are re-
markably short, but always very feeling, very
sweet. Be calm, very amiable. Learn to control your
feelings, or if not to control, to conceal them. Frequently angry feelings that are kept within your

bosom save you worse regret that frequently follows unguarded, hasty reply. Besides, it frequently places you in the position of finding all the wrong at 'he door of the other—the offending party it makes your friends. You say your friends find you very philosophical. You see I am always putting good lessons before you. My experience, dear Betsy, should be adopted by you. It has sound judgment to recommend it, and it is placed before you, as you only too well know, because I love you, and would save you much pain. My love to your mother, and tell her I am getting very home-sick. I want to take a quiet little dinner, with only three plates, and an old-fashioned talk and an old-fashioned time I would only too well love to have again, dear Betsy. My love and thoughts are all for you. Be kind and considerate, and all will be well.

HARRY.

LETTER XXVI.

*Letters from Betsy—He expatiates upon them—Waxes philo-
sophic—Longs to meet his beloved Petite—Italy—Advice,
etc.*

MARSEILLES, April 30, 1860.

MY DEAR LITTLE BABY:

I returned from Spain last night at midnight, and
at ten o'clock this morning found a big bundle of letters that had been accumulating here for the last four
weeks, and among all the rest it did not take me
many minutes to find no less than four from my
Betsy.   Some scolded, others were joyous ; some
were written with serious prose, others indulged in
sweet, smiling rhyme ; while still another inclosed
some humor—coming thus altogether.   To one not
somewhat versed in ordinary matters of human nature,
they would have found strange commingling of sor-
row and mirth, in pain and pleasure.   But, dear Baby,
I have seen rain from a black cloud whilst the sun
was shining.   I have seen a Baby, not my Petite, dry
up its little tears and be happy, and laugh almost in a
moment.   I have heard all the world complain, and
never yet found one single one who had not some one
complaint, or many, to make.   Why, dear Betsy, if I
could find one little mortal who would in all sincerity

say he or she was perfectly content, and wanted nothing, I would get down on my knees and cry.

No, dear Baby, I have tried so often to make you
comprehend this subject, and you won't ; you are so
very obtuse. Why, only look around. Your aunt
complains that the prayers of the good don't reach the
Cannibal Islands, and * * * complains that somebody
has depressed the price of lime ; * * * swears that
the Insurance Companies are a d— set of swindlers,
* * * complains of the dust, and * * * that * * * im-
poses upon him. Mr. Perry complains that stocks
are down, and Mrs. P—— wants to see her mother. Of
these all, none are so philosophic, so little disposed to
complain, as Aunty Shephard. She asks but that the
world will do her some little justice, and with good
health and an occasional visit from Bobby, Junior.
Thus, dear little Baby, the world goes on. You will
learn one of these days to take everything coolly, and
to smile at the great want of good sense and folly of
the big world. You will learn that the world is made
of a little sense and an ocean of poor simple things, who
have barely sense enough to put food in their mouths
after it is placed before them. You will learn that it is
the duty of every one to take care of himself first, and
in doing so to be guided by the thousand surrounding circumstances ; to listen and to pity the weakness
of others ; to not take offense at every word that is
said, but, on the contrary, to smile at often offensive
words, and inwardly say this poor innocent creature
knows not what she says. Dear Betsy, I always
preach to you, don't I, dear? I don't scold you, do
I, love ? I think constantly of you, dear Petite, and
I say how happy will my Baby be, when her Harry

4

returns once more to whisper good words of comfort to her.   Oh! Petite, the time begins to weigh heavily. I long to rest in quiet repose.   I long to live over again many sweet hours that are passed.   I long to see thee smile, and hear thy voice, and hear thee say thou art happy.   I am about to start for Italy, and there I will look towards the West, and turn towards home.   I could have written much about England, and France, and Spain, but always when I write to thee, I get on to those subjects that seem to trouble you needlessly, and I have seen so many people fret and worry, that I would have you learn now what you will learn later in life.

My love to aunty, and to thee, my dear little one, with all my heart, God bless you.

HARRY.

LETTER XXVII.

Wishes to be shut up with "dear, dear Baby"—Travel—A
sweet letter—Woman—A troubler—Moralizes—Excessive
love, etc.

BRUSSELS, July 14th, 1860.

MA PETITE CHERIE:

You see, dear Baby, I am constantly on the move;
indeed, so much so, that I am wearied beyond measure. I have undertaken to make a voyage of Europe,
and in one-fifth the time that is necessary to make it,
I am tired, tired, tired. I am wearied to that extent,
body and mind, that I would give worlds to be shut
up with thee, dear, dear Baby, and never know again
that man existed. We constantly hear of the tour of
Europe; and then it's lauded as being such a pleasure; yet I have not found one who, after making half
the tour, did not constantly desire that they were
again *at home*, at rest—somewhere; that they could be
entirely again within themselves, and again separated
from *all* of the world. Going, going, going; all the
time on the move—never at rest; to sleep, and to
have your sleep cut in two; to never do anything except with no satisfaction! Onward, onward; like the
Wandering Jew, always onward; no repose, no time
for thought; constantly getting new ideas, constantly

seeing new people, new customs, new associations of vast, immense importance—it creates such a confusion in the brain, that your thinking machine is worried, fatigued, tired out; you have no time to digest; it is a perfect dyspepsia, and the inward, physical man gives way in utter exhaustion!

I came express from Berlin and Hamburg, to find some letters; for since I was at Venice, some five weeks since, I have received nothing from anybody. You may know, dear Baby, how happy I was in reading your dear little letter. *This one* was a kind, sweet little letter, and made me ask the question, why you could not always write just such letters? I do not know why I deserve to be badly treated by you. I cannot understand why, because some anonymous correspondent writes to you, that I am to be made to suffer; but can readily understand that you are tired. I have been absent too long, and you are too precious to await my return; at least you have been asked to think so. But, dear Baby, I beg you never for one moment hesitate upon my account. Whenever you can do better, do it, and never have a thought of me. I am old, and growing gray; am worn out; past my youth, and to a sweet creature like yourself, past my value. The spring-time has gone, and the summer has rapidly approached the autumn. You have so many dear, valued friends, who would advise you; listen to them, and do what your best judgment dictates. I have done for you the best I could do, and have nought to regret; on the contrary, I feel satisfied I have been the kindest, best, sincerest friend you ever had. Again, dear, dear Mary, I say, never for one moment place me in the scale, when your real welfare can be advanced by leaving me out. I ask only to save you, nothing more. I placed you in a position where, had you had more patience, time would have worked out the rest; but this you would not comprehend. Oh, woman, woman! what a bundle of contrarieties! How many strange elements form thy soul! You are all weakness and all strength; you are all love and all hate; you can endure or you break down in a moment. Thus it is that you are the perfect heaven or hell of man's career. Dear Baby, I am disgusted that some wretch, some fiend, should have troubled himself to write to you that I was living too freely. Who could have been so very, very kind? Who could have had your interests and mine so much at heart? Who could have been so very, very honest, that he should have violated all ordinary honorable means to have advised you confidentially and anonymously that I was entertaining too many friends, or that I was entertained by too many or many of my many friends? But let him pass. The world is wretched. It is a little better than what we may expect hereafter. However, let us learn to be charitable; let us feel that the great mass of human nature is bad, very bad; and it is the more necessary that there should be some redeeming exceptions. Let us love our neighbors, and let us love and forgive our enemies, or rather our especial friends—the same thing. I am very charitable; I find it rather more comfortable to be so. I hate to hate. I am tired of knowing, and of having constantly thrust before me, how bad, how very bad the world is. I have long since found it out; and, God knows, I don't want to be continually reminded of it.

My love to your mother; and to yourself, my own

darling, darling Baby ; believe that I love you ever so much, or believe that I am a perfect impersonification of all that is bad ; I am prepared, fully hardened, to all that may be thought.   God bless you, my dear Baby.

HARRY.

LETTER XXVIII.

Germans—Thinks of his beloved—Nervous—Beer and smoke—
Wicked world—Letters,. etc.

BERLIN, July 21st, 1860.

MA CHERE PETITE :

Here I am, dear Baby, for once thrown completely
upon my own resources. I got along well with the
English, for they spoke a language that, with some
allowances, I could understand. With the French, I
got along, as you suggest, pretty well. With the Span-
iards, I had no difficulty. With the Italians, I made
myself understood. But since I struck Vienna, Prague,
Berlin, I am entirely lost. I can eat their smoked
goose, and know what is meant by Dutch cheese—it
speaks for itself ; but I do confess me, that their language is a little too much for me, just so much that I
cannot understand one single word. If there be any
one thing more lonely in the world than another, it is
to be just as I find myself at present. Why, you—
from your letters—may think it strange, but 'tis never-
theless true, I have thought of you, ever you, since
I have been here, incessantly ; so you cannot complain ; and had you been here, you would have learned
much of how far my adoration can go. In truth, and

in plain English, I am excessively nervous. It is now four weeks since, at Venice, I had letters; and it will be three or four days yet before I arrive at Hamburg, where my letters are now accumulating. If I could only speak Dutch, I would let it out, and drink beer, and smoke, and—and lose myself in a cloud of smoke and beer. But not speaking Dutch precludes the two latter, and I, forsooth, am doomed to despair. O! how much I ought to love human nature. There is so much that is charitable, and good, and just, in it. There is so much of the kind Christian; so much of love and feeling and good purpose in it. Had I not already seen so much, and expect so little, I might despair, and curse man as having lived beyond the limit after which any good may come; for hell, and hellish purposes, seem his only aim. Let him pass. A few good men—one in a thousand—must redeem the rest, or the world should stop, as having entirely failed in its destiny.

Adieu. My love to your mother. I am wearied and sick; my letters are strayed, and I am excessively nervous. I have heard nothing from Hamburg, from whence I expected letters from you. I leave here to-morrow for Hamburg, and shall thence go up the Rhine. Three or four weeks will find me in Paris. God bless you, dear Petite.

Your

HARRY

LETTER XXIX.

Sweet letters—Foreign customs—Wants to make Betsy happy
—Longs for home, etc.

LYONS, August 5, 1860.

MA CHERE PETITE:

I am-indebted for two sweet little letters received—
one in Zurich, and the other in Geneva; you have
many questions to ask in relation to my return. I
shall be in Paris in twenty-one days, and I shall cross
the Channel into England in two weeks or twenty
days, so that this certainly looks like coming nearer;
I am tired; worn out; old and gray; traveling as I
have traveled is hard labor; to travel for pleasure is
an impossibility. I have found no one yet that would
not be only too glad to get to a quiet, comfortable
home. I look upon traveling as upon hard study: the
information should be worth the labor after you shall
have expended it. After all, I like the French best;
there is more heart and willingness to oblige than about
any of the others. The Englishman invariably draws
his head in and shuts up his shell whenever he sees
anything approach him. The Frenchman approaches
you with his hand extended, and with a smile upon his
face. The Dutchman never removes his pipe, and his

heart is never moved until twenty-four hours after the occasion has passed. I have oceans of talk for you, and shall endeavor to make my dear Betsy the more happy that she has suffered so much. You are not the only one that complains; my brother-in-law says he has not received a word from me for sixty days ; indeed, Betsy, my little love, it is utterly impossible for me to write as I desire. I am so wearied that the moment I am left alone, not traveling, I immediately seek repose ; I want rest ; I want not only repose of body, but repose of the mind. The effect of constant occupation, although in the *extremely* desirable *pleasure* of sight-seeing, is fatiguing beyond what you would for a moment imagine. I expect the enjoyment hereafter, when I can find you in a happy mood for listening, and myself in a happy mood for talking. I have seen a great many interesting things, and many that were very curious and strange ; I have kept no journal, and, in consequence of my hurry, have much difficulty to prevent confusion. I will, however, endeavor to tell you a straight story, and to tell you everything that has occurred since I saw you. My love to your mother and to all, and with immense impatience I am dying to see you.

`Yours ever,

HARRY.

LETTER XXX.

Comstock — Joyous anticipations — San Franciscans — Mrs. Perry, &c.

PHILADELPHIA, Nov. 8, 1860.

BY DEAR BABY:

What do you think now? You see I have got back from Europe; my friends find me looking much better, but I find myself not feeling very well; we had an excellent passage, but I had with Comstock a berth the most forward in the vessel, and the motion kept me all the time uneasy. Since my return day before yesterday I have been kept busy receiving the friendly salutations of many friends, and I feel very seedy; I am very glad to get back, but shall be infinitely more glad when I have got back and received the welcome of still another dear little friend. Won't we be happy then, Betsy? I dread the voyage, it will be so very dreary and long—tedious. Well, Petite, what shall I say about myself—confess that I have not written quite so often as I desired, and have not received quite so many letters as I had hoped to have received? But never mind, I think that neither can complain much; I have written as often as it was practicable; you, I know, will not excuse or accept or believe any excuse or palliation I may offer, and I won't offer it. I am quite unwell this morning. I have a very unpleasant dizziness proceeding from the sea voyage, which unfits me for writing. I feel it my duty to write, and could not conscientiously be comfortable unless I do write. I see many from San Francisco and California, and all tell me that everything goes on well. I wonder how uncle's suit was determined? I shall call and see his attorney in New York. I hope the next time he tries any more malt liquor, he will insure against rascally insurance as well as against the elements.

Give much love to your mother; write until I request otherwise; sorry to hear Mrs. Perry has been so sick.

So with ten thousand good wishes, and ten times as many more sweet kisses, I am as ever, truly and sincerely

Your own

HARRY.

LETTER XXXI.

Sore throat — Capt. Small—Secession—Betsy—The lounge—
Nice little dinners—Some words about his beloved, etc.

PHILADELPHIA, December-11th, 1860.

MY DEAR BABY:

For the last week I have been quite unwell; my throat has annoyed me constantly. I have had an ugly attack of the rheumatism, and still more than all, I was worried because I had not written to you. This I am determined should be no longer. I wanted to get some information from your uncle's attorney, and wrote to him. He says the case awaits some return of a commission from California. He sent back to ask information of the whereabouts of Captain Small of the vessel, desiring to take his testimony. I got the best information I could, and in sending it to him, took the liberty of expressing my astonishment that it had not been taken long before. This is all I can send for your uncle. Well, my dear Betsy, what can I tell you? That all is fear and trembling here— nothing talked about but secession—all alarm, and fear, and panic—all praying for relief, and none to tell where it is to come from. I have as yet felt a conscious strength in our country, and cannot be made to

feel that there will be no compromise of all the
trouble.   I do not and cannot believe anything of the
kind.   One thing is certain: there is no longer any
crimination and recrimination that prevailed heretofore.   There is a most extraordinary respect spring-
ing up for the rights of others that had been most
shamefully forgotten heretofore; all are looking to
Congress for something to be proposed, and all feel
that if troubles are not precipitated upon us, that the
people alone, the first opportunity they have to speak,
would make all right.   Unfortunately, our guardian
angels, the politicians, have the matter in their hands,
and they have not the feeling nor the capacity to
master the subject.   They are pledged in the South
to secession, and they don't know how to avoid it.
But, my own dear little Betsy, what do you care about
secession, when one word of affection is worth all
the seceding States put together.   I have wished myself at home constantly of late, and I don't know
whether you remarked it, but I have been constantly
at the cottage, fully extended upon that little lounge.
Sometimes I think your mother must consider me a
very lazy drone, for I am seldom in her house that I
am not stretched out; but she knows that the only
pleasure, the only relaxation I have had for a long time,
from too many cares and too much trouble, was when
at the cottage.   Did not we have a good time, and a
good many of them?—didn't we enjoy all of those nice
little dinners, and then we always had such a nice
chat afterwards—and then that snoose after that?
Dear Betsy, how do you look?—like the picture?—
not so serious, I hope?—a little older? .None the
worse for that, I know.   Have you changed much?—

have you changed any? Will you be glad, very glad, to see me? These, and thousands of other questions, I ask and answer every day.

Some other questions I ask, which you can easily guess, and these are all sweet, dear questions. My dear Betsy, don't be angry with me: I will come soon, and then I will only be happy to see you perfectly so. My darling little one, ma chere Petite, my best wishes, my thoughts, my dreams, are always full of you.

My love to your mother, and for yourself an ocean full.

HARRY.

LETTER XXXII.

GOLDEN AGE, Wednesday, A.M.

MY DEAR, DEAR PETITE:

Thank God I am at last arrived, and will come to you at the earliest possible moment.

Much love,

HARRY.

LETTER XXXIII.

Out in the woods—The "war horse" faints—His shirts saturated—Commodore Watkins and lady, etc.

SAN JOSE, Sept. 11th, 1861.

MY DEAR BETSY:

I feel quite sure I shall spoil you in writing so often; but I thought, being unexpected, it would be the more agreeable. Well, then, my best, spoiled Baby in all of this Golden State.

I came near committing a great indiscretion. Yesterday I was very unwell, and suffered intensely. Yesterday afternoon I started my cattle, and after they were gone, I was afraid something might not go well, and determined to make all sure, so I started, overtook them, and went some six miles, where I intended they should pass the night. My friend was absent, and I was compelled to look for some other place. I went to a second and a third—it was night—and finally found a place, and started home. It was cold and damp, and I was stiff and suffering to that degree, that I had to be lifted out of my carriage. I took some hot soup, and whilst bathing my feet in hot water and mustard, I had the spirit lamps from my coffee machine lighted, and put under the chair upon.

which I sat, and the chair and all completely covered up ; it was some time before the perspiration started, but when it did begin, it poured off of me. Determined to have a good sweat, I sat until I grew deathly sick, and fainted ; this stopped any further steaming. I then added still other blankets, and stretched myself in a big armed rocking-chair, where, after drinking about a gallon of water, I got to sleep. I slept in the chair indifferently well, but with less pain than for a week. About two o'clock I found that my shirts were both completely wet, and getting cold. I changed and settled back in the chair, and remained there until morning. I then took a very warm bath in a quaker, and to-day feel better than at any time since I caught cold. I thought this news would be agreeable, and so write. I expect Commodore Watkins and lady, and am entirely unprepared to entertain them ; nothing that I wish—furniture and a dirty house, with table furniture to match. But the Commodore is a man of the world, and I will entertain him outside of the house. Good night ; pleasant dreams.

HARRY.

LETTER XXXIV.

At home—Sweets—Pillow-cases, etc.

SAN FRANCISCO, Sept. 21, 1861.

MY DEAR BABY:

I have just got home; would come immediately, but would not keep you at home on my account for the world.; will endeavor to come early, say eight to nine. Love to Aunt Mary; and am your much abused and innocent Lamb,

HARRY.

LETTER XXXV.

SAN FRANCISCO, May 18, 1859.

Hurra! Hurra!!

Hurra! Hurra!!

Hurra! Hurra!!

It never rains, but it pours!!

Hurra! Hurra!!

"The Elephants have arrived"!!

Hurra! Hurra!! Hurra!!!

The Elephants have brought their trunks with them!

Hurra! Hurra!!

I have found your trunk!!!

Hurra! Hurra!!

It will be delivered this morning. I have seen it with my own eyes! Would you believe it!! Hurra!!' Pray do.

Good morning, Betsy. Hurra!!!

HARRY.

LETTER XXXVI.

San Francisco, Wednesday, May 10.

MY DEAR MARY:

I am entirely recovered, and will come and see my Petite by or before two o'clock to-day.

Sincerely,

HARRY.

LETTER XXXVII

My Dear Baby:

I send by John, not Juan, some Sunday reading. Read—digest what you read—be happy, or at least be as happy as you can be. Remember me to Joe Taylor and his *two brothers*.

My love until we meet, and then again my love.

Harry.

LETTER XXXVIII.

TUESDAY, 9·A.M.

DEAR BETSY:

I will come at eleven A.M., and do all in my power to make you happy. I must go to San Jose.

Your

HARRY.

LETTER XXXIX.

WEDNESDAY, 6 A.M.

MY DEAR BABY:

I have been very sick all night. I was very sorry not to find you. Where was you? I want to go to San Jose, and must see you. I will come at 11. Don't go out, please.

Affectionately, your

HARRY.

LETTER XL.

SAN FRANCISCO, 3½ P.M.

DEAR BETSY:

I am up to my eyes in business.   Do not be angry
with me, but be indulgent until I can slip away.

Yours, sincerely, &c., &c.,

HARRY.

P. S.—We dine at six.   Behold the sparkling
and ice.

LETTER XLI.

DEAR CHARMER:

If you have had any of these, send it or them back. I am coolly writing some letters, having smoothed my face and made my inner person more comfortable by the close proximity of some cool, clean linen. A great institution is a clean shirt, isn't it? What are you doing? And what is Mrs. S—— doing? Tell her not to worry herself about the color of the fish. It was the fault of the flour, or of the lard, or something else; it was not hers, and it is useless to assume responsibilities not our own. If I could find out the man that ground that flour, or the hog that made that lard, then with propriety we might make heavy, serious accusation; but of this, more anon. Pleasant day; don't you think so? Many kind regards, and with a hope you may pass a quiet, tranquil day with the family, I shall rest in peaceful expectancy.

Au revoir. Thy " dearly beloved " who endeavors much to believe all you tell him,

                                        HARRY.

LETTER XLII.

MY DEAR MARY:

The top of the morning to you. My kindest regards with the bouquet for you, and I will come to see you at one to two, unless you are going out, of which send me word by William. My respects to your excellent aunt, and the package for your particular friend, Peter.

Yours, truly, &c., &c.,

HARRY.

Wednesday, 11 A.M.

LETTER XLIII.

My Dear Betsy:

I find it impossible to send you the information you desire.   I must bring it in person, excepting only that of the windows, for which we selected the large red flowers, and that is as you see below.

You will excuse me for saying no more, for it is already nine o'clock, and I have yet to go to town with this ; so, with many kind words for your dear mother, and much love for yourself,

I am, your

Harry.

LETTER XLIV.

DEAREST, DARLINGEST, SWEETEST BABY:

I hope you are perfectly well, and as happy as you deserve to be.

God bless you.

HARRY.

LETTER XLV.

My Dear Betsy:

God bless you. I have got home. If possible I will come up this afternoon; if not, expect me by 8 o'clock.

Send sheets and towels by the bearer; I send the pillow-case; the pin will indicate the length of the pillow. I hope you are exceedingly well, and as handsome and loving as ever. My love to your mother.

Your

HARRY.

LETTER XLVI.

Bushels of love—Heat—Mrs. Halleck, Mrs. Hepburn and
Mrs. Maxwell—Acapulco---Sweet Baby, etc.

ACAPULCO, Oct. 19, 1861.

MY DEAREST BABY :

Ten thousands of bushels of love to you ; I have
thought of you all the time, and every sigh and every
pulsation of affection has met with an immediate
response, and been returned as soon as it originated
with you. I have suffered much from the heat ; I
have kept my room every day until noon. I have
found it very necessary to revise all my military
studies. There has been much change. We have
very few passengers, but thirty-six in the cabin, and
with the exception of Mrs. Halleck, Mrs. Hepburn and Mrs. Maxwell, I have made no acquaintances. I have just written to Mr. Janes and Mr.
Scott—taking the business from the latter and placing
it with the former. I had intended to have written you
earlier this morning, but was too sick to do so. I
am now writing in the harbor of Acapulco, and am
fearful lest I may be too late for the mail bag ; and
now, my own sweet, dear Baby, my darling Baby—
who loves her own old Harry so very, very dearly—

sending you a heart brim full of love, with a corner, and that not a little one, for your dear, good mother, I must ever subscribe myself

Your own

HARRY.

LETTER XLVII.

Parting love—" Do you love me still ? "—Sacrifices " my own
darling Baby ! "—Small talk, etc.

STEAMER ST. LOUIS, NEAR PANAMA,
October 25, 1861.

MY OWN DEAR, DARLING BABY :

We will probably get across and start from Aspin-
wall to-night ; so that I will send my parting love, with
thousands of the dearest wishes for my own little,
sweet, dear Baby, who I know lives only in the sweetest memories of the past, surrounded by the uncertainties of the future, her little fears increased because
of her infinite love and faith in her own sincere, affectionate Harry. Dear, dear Baby, do you love me
still more than ever ? Will your love continue unabated ? Or will you permit some other to push between it and me ? Your happiness is in your own
hands. Your discretion, affection, and fidelity, will
be of your own choice, and your own conscience
must be your guide.

It pained me much, much more than I dared to
tell, to leave you ; but your kind resignation, your appreciation and approval of my conduct and the mo-

5*

tives which govein me, was to- me a source of great consolation.

We were so very, very happy ! You were every day more kind, more reasonable, more wise. All of the little rough edges that sometimes caused a passing shadow between us were gradually disappearing ; because, each loving the other so modified our conduct as to cause the least pain. And so let it always be ; never let either of us do anything that shall cause pain to the other, unnecessarily. I shall expect you to write to me at least every ten days. I shall keep you continually advised of everything important, and shall love you much more than you will believe. For my sake, do keep away from all such people as * * and * * . If you desire my love, you must make some little sacrifices to retain it; that is, if you consider it worth any such restriction. I am, in this, exceeding selfish, but only as you (if you love me so intensely as you have so often shown me) would have me be. My love makes me jealous of every favor, however small, you may extend to any other. The moment you find me otherwise, believe in my love no longer. But I am prolix, and have said enough. You have abundant discretion and judgment, when you choose to consult and are governed by them. I have suffered much. The voyage is intolerably long. I have wished for you thousands of times—yes, continually. I have muttered to myself, " my own darling Baby," by night and day. I have wanted you close, close to my heart. I have dreamed you *was* there, and that we were happy—happy as only we have been. Dear, sweet, darling Baby, love me always.

Give my love to your mother, and tell her she has no better, dearer friend than your Harry. Tell her to take the kindest care of you for my and her sake. Tell her you will be faithful to him who loves you only too dearly. Thine own existence and life,

HARRY.

LETTER XLVIII.

Amatory—Troops—Anxiety—Sighs for "Dear Betsy,"—etc.

WASHINGTON, November 9th, 1861.

MY OWN DEAREST, MOST DARLINGEST,
        MOST SWEETEST LITTLE ONE:

I commenced yesterday to write to you, but was interrupted. I commenced half an hour ago, and was again interrupted; so, now, with haste, for I have a friend to breakfast with me, and who I expect every moment, may make me again defer my duty—a duty which to me is sacred—a duty when not performed renders me unhappy, for you must know and feel, my own dear Baby, that your happiness to me is vastly more important to me than mine, and only believing you happy could I be content. Yesterday I passed seeing a review of fourteen thousand troops, and in the arsenals and offices. To-day I go across the river to visit the distribution of the Army along the Potomac. The next day I go to Philadelphia to complete my equipment; and then for work. At present, I go to Columbus, Ohio, where there are twelve hundred of my regiment waiting for me. I expect to be ordered either to Kentucky or to Washington—not yet determined. Do, my own little treasure, think of me constantly—feel and know that I love and am with you incessantly. Your separation from me is a constant pain. I have not yet a word from you. I am exceedingly anxious to hear what you have done since I left. Have you moved? Are you as content as a dear, little, reasonable being can be, separated from one who loves her? Do write to me every ten days; and let what will occur, never for a moment forget me or forget yourself. To your dear mother, say many things of friendship, esteem and love for me; for, as you must know, I have much, very much, affection for her. Kindest remembrances to your uncle. I would give my head to be with you, and to have one of our old-fashioned, happy breakfasts—that is, with the English muffins, and a nice sausage, and a cup of coffee. Dear, dear Betsy—dear, dear little love, you are more dear to me than ever. Be considerate and reasonable, and always true to your own faithful, affectionate

HARRY.

LETTER XLIX.

A sweet letter—The "war horse" sees a General—A love passage—He "loves" Betsy—"Take good care of my Baby," etc.

PHILADELPHIA, November 12th, 1861.

MY OWN BABY:

I cannot begin to tell you how happy I was yesterday upon the receipt of your dear, sweet, kind, loving letter. This had the genuine sound; it was fresh from a loving heart, whilst all of its impulses were brimfull of motion; whilst you could still feel the pulsation of my heart against yours, and my breath upon your cheek. 'Tis so sweet! I have read your letter over and over again. Do not forget, dear, darling Baby, how happy we were always—when you chose that we should be—when you did not get the fidgets, or do something to make me sad and miserable. I returned here on the night of the tenth, from Washington. I have visited all of the camps near Washington. Was presented on Saturday to General McClellan. He sent for me on Sunday, and said he should give me just such service as I desire. Told me to get ready at my leisure, see my friends, and return to him at Washington. I wrote to you three or four days ago. I am anxiously expecting another sweet letter from you. Do, my own dear love, write to me very often. Tell me that you love me still more and more, and nobody else. Tell me that I have absorbed all of your heart, and love, and thought. Tell me the truth; and I feel that my heart will be made happy. I know, as before, you will be told you are foolish in loving me; and those who say so will endeavor to convince you that you should love them. But, my Baby, you are older much than when we met; you have had some experience, and should long since have learned the difference between permanent good and transient pleasure. I love you, for yourself, and the great depth of my affection is in its concentration in thee. My love to your good mother. Tell her to take good care of my Baby; and under no circumstances allow her to expose herself. Remember me kindly to your Uncle Robert; and put your trust in him who loves you with all his heart and soul.

HARRY.

LETTER L.

"Dear little heart"—Love—Double distilled passion—Regiments — Will not expose himself—"Unnecessarily" — A caution, etc.

PHILADELPHIA, November 22d, 1861.

MY OWN DEAR, DARLING LITTLE ONE:

How can I describe the pleasure and intense happy thanks I feel for your loving *little* letter of the 29th of October, received to-day? Why, I have said to myself, ten thousand times since, that it is the very concentration of devotion—it is an entire volume of *pure*, plain, unembellished, intensified feeling, *pure*, fresh, from your dear little heart. No, that was unjust—it sprung directly from your great, big heart—made big, because of the superabundant love it bears her own dearly loved *mate*. Dear Baby, are we not well mated?—was ever man and woman more completely so? Have we not loved and loved, and grown lean and fattened on love? Have we not whispered love with all its sweetest accents, unintelligible but to the very, very few that have loved as we have loved? Have not all evil influences failed to part us—and has not all that they have done only brought us nearer together? My God! what would be this world if all were as happy as we have been?—

one continued spring-time of the heart's strongest confidence—oh! oh! dear, dear Baby! let it thus run on—be mine—let not even a breath divide us whilst life shall last; but let that abiding faith that *always* supports the Christian, support you and I in all affliction, and in that of all others that would be the greatest—that which would tend to separate us. I know you will be tempted, and believe me when I tell you I have unlimited confidence.

I love you, dear Baby! and oh, how intensely! and only equal to the intensity of my love would be my misery, and pain, and suffering, if my love was for one moment forgotten. Live on, love on, my dear one; listen not to bad counsels, it matters not from whom they come, but let the past remind you that the world is but a passing dream, and that you can rely on almost no one. Who has been to you always, from the first moment you first knew him, as faithful, as watchful, as truly devoted to you, as your own Harry? And who, in your cool judgment, will you believe will last and watch over you always, let what will occur, as he has done and will do? Dear Baby, God bless you. I love you, and my love is intense, because I feel that you are devotedly, exclusively, wholly mine, body and soul, mind and thought, night and day, and every hour of the day.

I have just returned from Ohio. There are but some five or six hundred of my regiment recruited; it will be six months before it will be full. I go to Washington to-morrow, to say I must have active service, or I will go home—I mean by home to you—for with you is all my pleasure—everything in which I have hope and love.

I can give you no news, for I know you have all of our news within twenty-four hours of its change. Direct as you now direct my letters. Have no fear that I will expose myself unnecessarily. Be but mine as always, and I will live for thee and the hope of making you happy.

My love to your mother; she is so very, very kind always to Harry. Tell her distance makes me love her only in proportion to its extent. Keep the curtains and keep my love closely locked in your dear, dear little heart — your little sweet, swollen heart, full of love always for your Harry.

Dear, dear, dear Baby, God, God will take care of you for your sake, for my sake, for our sakes.

Love, devotion, from thy

HARRY.

LETTER LI.

Disappointed—Gen. McClellan—A " sweet, dear little letter "—
A docile war-horse—War spirit—Wants letters, etc.

WASHINGTON, D. C., Nov. 29, 1861.

MY OWN DEAR LITTLE ONE:

The first impulse to me of any good fortune, is to feel that it will give one moment's happiness to my Baby, and it then becomes my duty to advise her of it, that I may feel that her little heart will be glad.

Well, Baby, in my last I wrote that I had been disappointed in my prospects at Columbus, and that there was no probability that my regiment would come into the field until next July. I returned here, and upon General McClellan learning the fact, he at once advanced me to the command of a brigade. I have not, as yet, been assigned to any command, but shall be soon. I shall complete my preparation within a week. I expect to be stationed not half a dozen miles from Washington ; probably not far from Alexandria.

I got a sweet, dear little letter, in which you tell me you had met with an accident. Your aunt knows how much this pained me. Be more careful ; don't do so again, dearest. I have not heard from a single person, but yourself, in San Francisco, and am, of course, in ignorance of all my affairs. I hope my best friend, your mother, is perfectly well, and as contented as a lady, who likes sometimes to scold a little bit, can be. Do you know, my Baby, that I could live with your mother forever, and never have an angry word with her! She has the best old heart in the world, and her impulses are of the most generous character.

The war spirit is unabated, and the Government is gradually becoming very strong. But still the end is not yet, and we must wait patiently. I suppose your uncle is engaged in business, and I sincerely hope, successfully. I hear but little of San Francisco, or California. Indeed, I am entirely out of the way of it, and shall be still more so. Don't fail to write me, *at the very least*, every ten days. Direct as before, to Philadelphia, Pa. And now, my Baby—my own dear Baby—with millions of love,

I am, truly, thy

HARRY.

LETTER LII.

Sick to see Betsy—Vanity—Wants war—Love talk—Warm clothing—Defines his position—Dreams—The war-horse and English muffins, etc.

PHILADELPHIA, December 15, 1861

MY OWN BABY:

Your sweet, dear little letter, of November 8th, was received a few days since, and went straight to my heart, and made it ever so glad. .I am so very sorry that your hand is still so painful. Do get well. I am sick to see you. You are my only cause of anxiety. My health is excellent; I never weighed so much in my life, and all of my friends congratulate me upon my appearance—not that I am handsome, but healthy, which to my Baby is vastly more important.

I am much disappointed that I have not yet been ordered into the field. My name has not yet been sent to the Senate; indeed, none since those appointed up to August. General McClellan and my friends say that all is right.

My love, my Baby—my Baby love, my little thing, my all—yes, all to me—do you love me as much as ever, more than ever? Do you remember that you assured me, over and over again, that you had only known happiness and extreme pleasure with me? Why, my little sweetheart, ours was a continual, increasing love. You sometimes scolded me unjustly, but I never retorted ; and when you found you had done your Harry an injustice, you told him so, and we loved each other the more, didn't we, love? Don't you think our love was entirely too primitive? It was not fashionable ; we were always too much in earnest, and our hearts were always in it. Dear Baby, do write to me oftener. I have but three letters from you. I have written, I believe I love you most. I don't say so much about it ; but mine is more regular, less impulsive. What do you think about it? Tell me ; you can write to me without restraint. I have abundance of warm clothing. I got them because 'twas your desire. I am sorry you are alone. I don't want you to be alone ; and I don't want you to have any male visitors. You understand me. You have only to ask yourself, what would Harry advise? and you could always respond. I don't mean you, I mean your heart ; for it loves and thinks of me—dreams of me. Dream sweet dreams, until we can dream together. Give my love to your mother. Did you give her the extract I sent you for her, regarding the last burial of her dear, patriotic friend, Patrick McManus?

How I do want some of the English muffins—the best ever made in or out of England. Love, love, love, now and always to my dear, dear Baby.

HARRY.

LETTER LIII.

General McClellan—The "war horse" impatient for the field—
Latham—"Dear, dear Baby"—Love intense—Advice, etc.

PHILADELPHIA, Jan. 8th, 1862.

MY OWN SWEETEST BABY IN ALL THE WORLD:

I am annoyed beyond measure. I advised you of
what had been done, and of the kind, friendly disposition of General McClellan. Since that nothing has
been done. Gen. McC. has been ill for three weeks
and is unable to attend to my business, and my
appointment sticks fast, and I have been waiting in
unquiet expectancy. I have made all my preparations ; my servants, horses, equipments, all are ready,
but I cannot act without a commission. Well, Baby,
you know how much such uncertainty would annoy
me. I am cross, depressed, company for nobody, and
less so for myself; have wished ten millions of times
that you were near me. I would shut myself up with
you, and never leave your kind influences until something reasonable was done. Mr. Latham has been
exceedingly kind to me, but the holidays interrupted
everything; all have sought their pleasures but poor
me, and with me it would have been a sacrilege,
for my Baby is not here. Dear, dear, dear Baby,

how often, how incessantly I think of you, and am
with you. Had I anticipated so much difficulty, I
should have stayed and nursed you—made you happy.
This would have been so easily done, for in my
presence alone you were always so. Do you ever
forget me? Do you always think of me? Do you
never allow yourself for a moment to think of any one
else? Forgive me, dear, dear, dear little one; but I love
intensely, and the mere thought that for one moment
you could listen to another, would make me miserable,
indeed. I know you well and alone. I do not
believe that all of the world could make you forget me
for one moment. I am exceedingly depressed to-day,
and nothing but my love for you—the all-absorbing
love for you—gives me courage to write. Indeed,
not having written for ten days, I was daily becoming
more miserable and unhappy, for I knew you would
be expecting a line—an assurance of my warm, heart-
feeling love—love with all that Nature intended we
should feel who love as we have loved, dear, dear, my
own dear little one. God bless you, and bring us
soon together; for as you so often say, so say I, our
separation is painful, cruel, unnatural—Nature made
us for each other. Love to your mother and uncle,
and let calm, good reason and judgment govern all you
do. Whenever you are in doubt, think of me, your
own dear, darling

                                        HARRY.

LETTER LIV.

In the field—Harry in the saddle—He prophesies—A great General—English muffins—Kisses—Tents, etc.

HOOKER'S DIVISION, NAGLEE'S BRIGADE, }
March 3d, 1862. }

MY OWN PET:

Your dear little sweet note gladdened my heart of a cold, wet, disagreeable day, and made me feel ever so happy. Here I am, dearest, at last. Just two weeks ago I was told to prepare and come immediately here, which I did, getting here on the following day. Since that time I have been expecting constantly to be brought into the field of most active service. The enemy are within two miles and a half of where I am writing. Our pickets on the bank of the Potomac frequently halloa at each other, and there is hardly a day we do not exchange courtesies, by way of an iron messenger sent rather unceremoniously into each other's camp. We expect to cross the Potomac very, very soon; after which, of course, the utmost vigilance will become constantly necessary, and we expect some lively work. I have an excellent brigade— two regiments of Massachusetts, one New Hampshire, and one Pennsylvania—and have great confidence that they will do great credit to themselves. I have

6

constant, most laborious occupation, frequently out all
day, and until two, three, four o'clock in the morning
in the saddle. My own Baby, does she want to
see her Harry?—does she want to make love and be
exceedingly happy?—does she want to breathe love,
feel love, whisper love, and feel beloved? Courage,
my dear Betsy, time rolls around rapidly, and the war
will soon end. The Fourth of July will see all ended,
and then—and then—and then—I know two persons
will rush into each other's arms! Don't I? Won't we
love each other even more than ever, if possible?
That cannot be, for we had learned to drink the cup
sweetened to the utmost. Give my love to your dear
mother, for she is really one of the best, dearest, kindest
darlings that ever occasionally got vexed, and always
smiled upon me—ain't she, love? Never mind, let us
live upon the memories of the past, and upon the
expectations in the future. We will be the more
happy, that our affections and love are so painfully
tried. Do you think, love, you would have loved me
half as much if I had not been absent from you?
Don't you rather think the absence increases and
learns us how much we are really necessary to each
other? Write to me, as heretofore, to Philadelphia,
but you may address General Henry M. Naglee. I
am very agreeably surprised to find that my duties
come very naturally to me, and so far have had no
difficulty; on the contrary, although but two weeks
here, I have succeeded in completely capturing the
confidence and respect of all of my officers, and am
received in the most flattering manner by all. Tell
my good old aunty that she must not make all of the
English muffins until I come; they were so good—I

mean my kind. Didn't we have such nice little breakfasts, and were we not happy, all three of us? I do
like that old, good mother of yours so much ; as Robby
would say, she is so kind to me, and gives me so
many good things, and shows always so much care
and concern for me. I only wish I could hear her
laugh, just one hour—yes, ½ an hour, ten' minutes—
yes, I would almost be content with one kiss of my
Betsy ; I mean one of our kisses—kisses, in which
heart and soul and heaven all seem commingling in
sweet embrace. I hear very seldom from Mr. Janes,
scarcely ever ; indeed, you are the only one with whom
I have any correspondence. I sometimes get a business letter, but none of a friendly nature. Yours are
so dear, so very full of love and devotion, and sweet
memories of the past, so sincere and earnest, why
should I not be happy, knowing, feeling the positive
conviction that you are devotedly, faithfully, wholly
mine, body and soul, and mind, and heart and all. I
am just getting my tents in comfortable condition, but
expect to be compelled to move within three days.
If anything important transpires, I shall at once
advise you ; so be of good cheer, and live on and love
as ever, with your entire heart, your own darling,
devoted

HARRY.

Give my kindest remembrances to uncle.

H——Y.

LETTER LV.

Rain and sentiment—Potomac—The war-horse likes service—
Politicians—Abolitionists—War life—Hooker—The war-
horse " too strong for him"—Love talk, etc.

HOOKER'S DIVISION, FIRST BRIGADE,
March 15, 1862.

MY DEAR BABY :

It is raining as though the deluge was about to be
repeated. My tent is dripping in every direction. I
have shifted my writing three or four times to find a
place free of drops. I am entirely alone, and I just
now asked myself what could I do, and what do you
think popped into my head, and it was just the simplest idea in the world ; and it was that, raining pitch-
forks, and dark, and gloomy, and heavy, and forbid-
ding, I would be perfectly happy in one place only,
and where do you guess that would have been ?—but
one in the world, and that with you, where no one
would disturb us, where we could have talked and
loved, and be happy as only we have been happy ; and
then I said that cannot be, for I am down on the
Lower Potomac hunting rebels, and you at San Francisco, counting the hours when your Harry will love
you again ; and then your good spirit suggested, Well,
if we cannot be happy together just now, you can

write to your Baby,.and that will be the next good thing you can do, and behold you have the letter. I am well and busy, expecting every moment to be ordered down the Potomac. The prediction I made long since that the war would terminate by the 4th of July, will be fulfilled. They are coming in rapidly, and I am sick of it; not that I do not like service —on the contrary, I am perfectly charmed with it; but I am disgusted with the outrageous interference of politicians in the conduct of the war. They are determined to introduce abolition into the war, and make officers of the army aid them in their hellish purposes. I get along quite well in camp. At first it was very hard. I got the rheumatism; the fare was bad, my bed was bad, everything went by contrast; but I have mended matters much. I have my own servants, a good cook included. I have enlarged my quarters. I have made my bed more soft; but still there is much, Petite, wanting in it. But with all I have not a moment to myself. I seldom get to bed until very late, and always get up an hour before it begins to be light.

This is the only way I can keep the machine at work as I like to see it work. Confidentially, that is, for your ear and that of your mother, one of my troubles comes from the fact that Hooker is inefficient; he is slow, and not capable. I came a long ways, and for the purpose of doing something. I come in contact with him often. I am too strong for him. My opinions receive favor at Washington, and to the condemnation of his plans. He is envious of me, but is afraid to oppose me. Our intercourse on my part is frank, candid, and determined to do everything to carry out the good purposes of the service ; his, on the contrary, is shy, spiteful if I leave for a day, and evidently not satisfactory to himself ; yet he dares not say I am not a superior officer, and that if I have a chance I will not make a mark.   From this you will appreciate the disagreeable point of my duty.

My love to your good mother, and to Uncle * * * ; and to you, what words shall I use—none equal to my *desires*, not warm enough ; none enthusiastic, devoted, full, round, satisfactory, to make you feel how much, how very, very much I love you.

HARRY.

I got a sweet, dear little letter from you two or three days since.   H.

LETTER LVI.

Yorktown—Bullets—Sweet letter—Love rampant—The war-horse and his brigade—Glory—Asks Betsy to dream of him, etc.

CAMP WINFIELD SCOTT, VA., NEAR YORKTOWN, }
April 20, 1862. }

MY BABY :

Your dear little letter of February 24 was received only yesterday. I almost despaired of ever hearing again from anybody, for it had been ten weeks since I had received a letter. Here I am, hard at work before Yorktown, all being engaged in the preparations for the assault of the heavy works that form so defiantly before us. We expect hot work, but feel great confidence in the results. I took a little turn a few days since, and examined all of the works of the enemy. Had a delightful, interesting day of it. Heard the occasional whistle of an unfriendly bullet, but was not harmed. Your sweet little letter filled me with the most loving sensation ; indeed, for a time I forgot all military aspirations, and would have given worlds to have jumped into your dear little arms. Baby, you are a dear little creature, at least so to me, and what care I for more than that ? You are kind to me, and love me, and always were most happy when I was near to you, and most unhappy when absent from me. I have suffered lately from excessive heat and hard labor. There is no one who works harder than myself, and I am most happy to know that it is appreciated. I have made hosts of friends, and my brigade, although at first did not like me, now exhibit continually evidences of their entire confidence and esteem. My staff officers never tire. Night and day they endeavor to relieve me of my labors, and I am assured they are entirely devoted to me. All this, dearest, is gratifying in the extreme, and sweetens the bitter necessity of my absence from you, and the extreme labor of an active military life. I am in for it now, as you know, and I shall hope for the best, and will promise you, if I do not gain glory I shall under no circumstances leave the army with fewer friends than I had when I entered it. Dear Betsy, say many dear things to your dear mother for me; repeat what I have so often said and written to her, for as you know, I love her dearly. Be ever so good; think constantly of me; dream always of me alone; and hope for happiness, extreme happiness, whenever we meet again. Write often, don't wait for letters; but adopt some rule, and always comply with it—say every week or ten days. Would not that be little enough, dear, sweet, loved one?

I am, devotedly, your own darling

HARRY.

LETTER LVII.

In the swamps—Quinine—Reconnoissance—Battle of Williamsburg—Sumner—Keyes—Self-praise—Richmond—Torpedo—Battle Ground—Hooker—Remarks—Janes—Sweet Words, etc.

CAMP, 27 MILES EAST OF RICHMOND, }
May 16th, 1862.

MY DEAREST, DEAREST PET:

I have not written for two weeks—so long, that I cannot longer be contented until I shall have done so. I have been for the last six weeks in the swamps between the York and James rivers—not sick, not well—much sickness around us; but I have been exceedingly careful of myself, for I am only too anxious to be happy with you again. I take quinine constantly, drink very little, eat nothing, and that of the simplest character. Frequently I get nothing in a long march from morning until night but a hard cracker and a piece of cold pork; and frequently am out all night in the rain—without a tent, without a blanket—standing all night—everybody under arms in his place, expecting an attack.

We have had some hard fighting. I have worked hard, but as yet not happened to be at the right spot. I made a very creditable reconnoissance on the 29th of

6*

April, in which quite a number of my people were
killed. Was in the advance on Sunday preceding the
battle at Williamsburg ; but on Monday, Sumner and
Keyes held my command in reserve all day until
McClellan came up, when he sent me to support our
troops that had turned the works on the left of the
enemy. When I came upon the ground, the enemy
gave way, and we did not get into the fight. I am
happy to say to you, my own dear little one, that I
have made crowds of friends with all of the promising
officers, and that my command have unlimited confidence in me. We expect a hard fight at Richmond,
which may come off at any moment. Gen. McClellan
is here, and we have a superior army of about
120,000. The enemy will concentrate 170,000. But,
my own dearest, darling little one, who is only so
excessively happy when nestled in the arms, upon the
breast of him she loves, what do you care for all these
things ? I am almost afraid to tell you, that my horse
rode over one of the torpedoes the enemy had buried
in the middle of the road we had to march over to
occupy their batteries at Lee's Mills, near Yorktown.
It exploded immediately after I had ridden over it,
and killed and wounded seven men. The killed were
mangled in the most horrible manner ; their legs were
torn from their bodies, and the flesh of their thighs
from the bones, and. the joints all separated. The
battle-field at Williamsburg was marked by a great
many dead and wounded. The enemy lost about one
thousand, and from what I can learn, we lost not less
than two thousand five hundred. Hooker's men were
slaughtered ; and it is said many more were killed, in
consequence of the confusion, by their own balls, than

were killed by the enemy. I am inclined to believe that the enemy got the best of it. They were inferior in numbers to us. Our men fought well. Too much censure cannot be thrown upon those in command.

If McClellan had not come upon the ground, we should have been beaten—this is *entre nous.* Write me a sweet, dear little letter, full of love. Tell me when you love and think of me most; tell me whether you sleep well, and whether you ever dream of me. I never hear from Janes, or anybody else at San Francisco, but yourself. Again, dearest little angel of my devotion, upon whom I concentrate all my love, and all of my desire, let us hope to be soon, very soon, happy—excessively happy together.

Your own

HARRY.

LETTER LVIII.

Sighs for Betsy—Love superior to Schells—An extract—The
Tribune—The war-horse among the splinters—"Three
horses killed"—Sick soldiers—The hero takes care of his
health—Colonel Bailey—New York Artillery—Naglee's
Brigade—Loving words, etc.

CAMP NEAR RICHMOND, NAGLEE'S BRIGADE, }
                June 21st, 1862.   }

MY OWN DEAR BABY:

You don't know how often I think of you. When
lying upon the wet ground, unable to sleep lest
neglect might lead to disaster, I have forgotten the
dreariness and exposure, and filled my mind with you.
When midst the horrors, and rattle, and thunder of
war, I thought of only my Baby. When the air all
around me was filled with iron and lead, I thought of
my Baby. When the ground seemed opening under
me, and shell coming from beneath it, then, too, Baby,
I thought of you. And then, when for two weeks I
kept my bed, I would have given a dozen worlds, had
I possessed them, for one dear sweet kiss of my dear,
dear, little one. I send you an extract taken from the
Tribune of 16th instant. We have been most grossly
maligned; but I am so accustomed to such treatment
that I found I was much less annoyed than others,

knowing that the truth would come, and that the dead would speak for the living. Now the flood is in the other direction, and there is a disposition to give us all the credit we are entitled to. I was required in my position to be in advance, and consequently very much exposed. A rifle ball scraped my right nipple, and a shell struck me in the small of the back, just under my right shoulder blade. Two shots struck my right leg, and I had five balls strike three horses, all of which were killed or abandoned by me. On the 24th, one week before, I had a splendid bay horse shot. But, dear, dear Petite, a miss is as good as a mile, and we will meet again, and be ever so loving, ever so happy. We are now preparing for another grand struggle. It will be desperate on both sides, for our men fight now without fear, and the enemy fight through desperation. I can form no idea when the war will terminate, certainly not sooner than I wish. Both sides are sick of it, and would willingly see the end of it. My brigade has suffered much from sickness. Of 6,600 men, over 3,000 are sick and wounded. I went into the fight with 1,600 men, and lost over 638. This is called heavy fighting. I have now been nearly four months in the field, living I will not distress you by telling you how. *All* of my staff are sick ; more than half of them compelled to go away. Frequently I am in the saddle from 2 A.M. till dark, and allowed to sleep just when the enemy will keep still for an hour or two. Frequently I go to bed at 4, 5, and 6 o'clock P.M., completely exhausted, and at 11 and 12 P.M. suddenly sent out to the extreme front, to provide for some attempted surprise.

But, Baby, *I take my bath every morning*, and think
of you, so that, dear Baby, although I have exposed
myself in battle, I have taken all kinds of precau-
tion to save myself from sickness. I have an excellent servant, and he watches me incessantly. He
comes into my tent and covers me up, and makes
gutters to keep my tent from being flooded. It has
rained almost constantly. I do want some vegeta-
bles ; I want an onion ; I want a good potato. I am
tired of beef. I live on hard bread and some dried
peaches. Occasionally I have some pork ; I like fat
pork. And the greatest treat I have had for a long
time was of a hot day at 12 M. I had a little box of
dried figs, and with some fresh water and a little nice
whisky, it was to myself and friend a great pleasure.
This was Colonel Bailey, of the First New York Artillery. The fight commenced soon after, and before
two hours he was shot dead through the forehead
close by my side. Ever so much love to your mother,
and to your Uncle * * *. Tell him for me that Naglee's Brigade made the best fight of any during the
war. The loss of the enemy was about 10,000, that
of our army about 6,000. Well, Baby, do you think
of me often, as often as when with you, as often as
when I tried so often to be your own darling, and you
used to scold me ? But, dear little sweet partner of
my pleasures, I was not so very, very bad. Yes, let
me see ; once, that election night—little tight then,
wasn't I ? I am waiting anxiously to get another dear
little one of those sweet little *billet doux*. I feel happy
the moment my fingers touch the seal, and I feel all over
when you assure me of your constant love and happi-

ness when with me. Once more, my own little one, *body* and *soul* are all mine.

Your own dear, darling, loving

HARRY.

LETTER LIX.

A letter from Betsy—Richmond—Battles—He wants rest—
Halleck—Economy—Janes and "indebtedness."

PHILADELPHIA, July 31st, 1862.

MY DEAR BABY:

Your dear, darling, sweet little letter, of June 22d,
was just received ; and I must confess you are becoming the most considerate, reasonable little love that
ever lived. You fully appreciate the constant occupation that surrounds me ; and when in the field, the
utter impossibility of writing a dear, sweet, darling
letter, the only one I would like to send to her who
loves so very, very much. You have long before this
heard of the dreadful fighting before Richmond, and
that your Harry received much credit for the part he
took in the many trials between the armies. I have
escaped most miraculously. I know my Baby will
read, with tears in her eyes, the descriptions of our
many sufferings and of the carnage on both sides. I
send you a copy of my report. I have not published
my reports of my reconnoissance at Bottom's Bridge,
nor the fight at White Oak Swamp, nor at Williamsburg, nor at several other places. Indeed, I want rest.
I have been entirely exhausted ; my nervous system

gave way, and I have been endeavoring to recruit it, and am much better.

What shall I say to your mother—that I am much obliged for the letter? Of course I am; and tell her I shall not require her to address my dear " General," but that between us, Harry is quite as well understood.

Halleck has been placed in command of all the land forces of the U. S., and it has given much confidence. I cannot predict the future, but preparations are making for still more desperate efforts. Much fighting has yet to be done, and much honor yet to be won.

I wish I was at home. I wish I was with you. I wish I could make you ever so happy; I would only be too happy to do it. Never mind, time will soon roll on, and then we will have the experience of the past to guide us, and nothing will again tempt me to leave a peaceful, quiet, and happy life. I did get the letter of Mr. Janes, of eleven pages, but it is the only letter I have received from him. I have been living very economically. I have drawn no money from Janes, and hope he is paying off my indebtedness.

And now, with bushels of love, I am truly, lovingly, devotedly,

Your own darling

Harry.

LETTER LX.

Remarks on the "situation"—Love by multiplication—Halleck—Fremont; he is "played out".—"West Point men," etc.

NEW-YORK, August 16th, 1862.

MY OWN BABY DEAR:

I wrote to you not long since, but forgot to put "steamer" on it, and fear it may miscarry. I am at present recruiting, and begin to feel in pretty good training—ready for the fray. The new position of our forces will place us in a much more favorable country for movement, and out of the swamps that have caused us so much destruction. Well, Baby, shall I tell you how much I love you? Just multiply yours by one thousand, subtract nothing, and add an ocean full, and that won't begin to approximate. Indeed, the only way you can appreciate it, will be to feel it; that would be more satisfactory to both. You said something in your last about writing every week, but as yet I have no evidence of it, and am really afraid you forgot your excellent resolution even before it was scarcely born. You know you held me under close subjection—shall I say subjugation, or, rather, shall I say, lovely restraint, or restraint—only because I loved my Betsy, and my Betsy loved me.

Ah! them's um ; that's the kind—yes, kind is the word, and kind was the feeling always. Really, dear Baby, from the word "go," have we not always considered each the happiness of the other more than anything else? You did accuse me of being vain, but never of being selfish in my love for you. No, it was ever generous, pure, the full gush, given freely from my heart—'twas all thine—and you, greedy, took it all, and wanted more. In this you was selfish, for you never would consent to any division. Give my love to your mother and Robert ; tell him by the time he gets this, if we are lucky, the end will be nearer. Halleck is doing well. Fremont is played out, and people do say West Point men make pretty good soldiers. Write ; love me ; be happy, and I will bless always my Baby,

HARRY.

LETTER LXI.

Depressed—Love in a garret—The army to be "left alone"—
Sweet words to Betsy—Love and War—Love, etc.

WASHINGTON, Sept. 6th, 1862.

MY OWN DEAR, SWEET PET:

I cannot tell you how much I await a letter; and to
estimate how very, very much I want to see you, and
feel that you are near and with me, would require
great comprehension. I am quite depressed. Everything goes wrong, and we are shamefully defeated,
and our defeat, we all know, is in consequence of the
entire worthlessness and utter wickedness of those at
the head of the Government. Oh! how many times
have I said to-day, "My own dear, dear little Love,
what would I not give to see her—what would I not
give to have her here?" Indeed, I should have liked
to have disappeared with you in a garret, or in a
cellar—anywhere, providing only the world should be
shut out and we be shut in. The Lord only knows what
will be the result of it all—nothing but disgust stares
all in the face, and yet none doubt our ability—the
certainty of immediate success—if the army is only
left alone.

Dear, dear Betsy, how much I do love your own

dear, dear, sweet little self. My heart to-day is so full of you, that I am really miserable. I want to hug, and kiss, and love you, and cover you all over with endearing caresses. Oh! how much doubt hangs over everything, and imbecility surrounds all. There is incapacity, great abundance of it, everywhere in and out of the army. Dear Baby, do you love me?—do you love only me? Have you not a thought, an inclination elsewhere? Have you, midst the absence, and silence, and uncertainty of war, loved only me? How bitter the separation—how sweet the consolation—how excessively happy our meeting, love! Love to you, love to your dear mother—love to you—love to you—love to all who contribute to the *real* happiness of my Baby.

Her

HARRY,

LETTER LXII.

"Bless her little soul"—Cold—Yorktown—Secesh scarce—A love fit—Desires—Advice—Wants a long letter, etc.

YORKTOWN, October 6th, 1862.

MY OWN DEAR LITTLE ONE:

Your sweet little comfort was received here a few days since, and went straight to my heart, and there, after causing me to exclaim repeatedly, "Bless her little soul! how very, very happy we make each other," it was sacredly filed away, as an additional solace and assurance that there is at least one little thing worth living for.

It was quite cold this morning, and although my camp bed is not quite as wide as myself, I could not help thinking of our happy memories, and the reverie was delicious in the extreme; and how vastly in contrast with all around me—nothing but hard, rigid, military duty. I have here some six or seven hundred troops, and although fully prepared for the enemy, there is no enemy within thirty miles, and there will be none. I almost think I heard you exclaim, "Thank God! I hope he will remain there." Oh! you selfish little mortal, you would have nothing to occur that should prevent the rush to arms that will occur when we come in close contact with each other. I expect to find a dear, sweet, soft, tender little virgin, with her cherry lips brimfull of honey, breathlessly waiting, waiting to be completely annihilated with love.

But let us for a moment forget the intensity of our love, and return to some calm reason. Your dear letters give me much consolation, and the more so, that from one to the other I trace the maturity, the improvement, resulting from experience and thought. You are more contented; you look with more reason upon circumstances that surround you, and appreciate the necessity of my absence. Indeed, it will not be long ·before I shall first advise with you before I determine for myself. You have learned much experience at an early age; you have seen that the world has more misery than happiness in it; you have learned that you will find but few that you can rely upon— many to promise, and look and show much promise, and that in the end were unworthy. You have learned to love your darling, and only because you have found that after years of experience and trial, you can rely implicitly upon his word and upon his love; and that the more you have seen and been with him, the more you know that your past happiness has been identified with his. Do write me often, and send me a long letter, boiling over with love. Kindest affection to your mother; tell her all manner of good things for me, for you and she know I love her.

Your own dear, darling

HARRY.

LETTER LXIII.

Fever—Death of Mr. Janes—Etting Mickel—Wants to kiss
Betsy—"Old Keyes"—Mrs. Bissell—No love, etc.

YORKTOWN, December 2, 1862.

MY OWN DEAR PETITE:

I have been quite sick with an attack of the typhoid
fever, but am again well and ready for active service,
which I fear will not be soon. I have been held here
doing nothing, looking on, cursing and growling at
the excessive vanity and stupidity of old Keyes.

I do not see that we have advanced one foot during
the entire campaign, and results seem to me exceedingly doubtful. I was shocked at hearing of the
death of Mr. Janes. He was happy in his home, and
his business position and business relations were all
that he could have desired. I telegraphed to you
upon the receipt of your letter ten days ago. I have
written to Mr. Etting Mickel, to provide for your comforts, etc. You will, I know, be pleased with him.
He is an excellent man, and a friend that I appre-
ciate highly. How very much I want to see you. I
want to kiss you; I want to love you; I want to
make you happy all over. But we must wait a little
longer. He who makes nations will determine our

existence as one or two nations to carry out the great objects of creation. It is raining, and a gloomy, ugly, heavy day. I hate old Keyes. Who don't? By-the-by, he got married the other day to Mrs. Bissell, and came away and left her in Baltimore. Do you think they will be happy? She won't like Keyes: he is too detestable for any one to like, and she loves herself and her pleasures ever to trouble herself about him. There won't be much of a honey-moon—not such as we know something about.

I can give you no news, for there is none. My time is entirely taken up with military duty, and we are trying to get ready to pass the winter at Yorktown. Love to your mother, and am all over, your dear old darling.

God bless you.

HARRY.

LETTER LXIV.

He grows unhappy — Keyes — Gen. Foster — Love — Janes — Scott — He is a " monitor " — A " rash man " — Keyes " chicken-hearted " — Hooker — Heintzelman — Peck — McDowell and Sumner—" Spooney "—Bombast—" Love on—love ever."

NEWBERN, N. C., Jan. 12th, 1863.

MY OWN DEAREST LITTLE SWEET PET:

Every day have I found myself growing more unhappy, and it was because I did not write to you. Every morning I said " 'tis a shame I do not write," and my heart fell sick, and, in fine, sadness and real unhappiness has taken possession of me. I cannot delay longer. I cannot excuse myself, except that I had been, under Keyes, excessively annoyed, disgusted, fretful. Since here commanding a Division, and commanding the Department of N. C., in the absence of Gen. Foster, I have been much engaged, but I have a clearer sky above me, and prospects in the future.

Don't for one moment believe I forget you, for it is not true. I think of you incessantly. I would have you on this side, but you would incessantly worry, because you would imagine me in danger.

The death of Janes has been a source of great regret to me, and the refusal of Scott to take charge of my business disconcerted me. I had discharged Scott because of his conduct to you.

Withal, I am in good health, work hard, have made and make many military admirers, for they look upon me as a kind of monitor that may run against anything without being hurt. Keyes says I was the most rash man that he ever saw. I say that Keyes is as much out of his element as that noted hen that sat upon duck's eggs, and in my estimation is much more chicken-hearted—infinitely more selfish. Enough of him! Thank God, I am now entirely beyond his influences, and whilst his star is in the mud, mine slowly ascends, and will yet shine when Keyes, Hooker, Heintzelman and Peck—all made by stealing my credit—are forgotten. These men, with McDowell, Sumner and others, have got beyond their depth. By slow degrees, truth will out and justice will be done. Love, much love, to your own dear mother. Tell her much to console and comfort her ; tell her to fear not, I have friends wherever I command, and my soldiers will follow me unto death. Dear Pet, shall I say I write with a heart brimful and overflowing?—yours must assure you of it. Then, love on—love ever,

Your

HARRY.

LETTER LXV.

Home-sick—"Sweet, sweet love!"—The war—No letters
Dying to see Betsy—A bad attack of sentiment.

HARBOR OF BEAUFORT, N. C.,
January 26th, 1863.

MY OWN DEAR PETITE:

I have been full of you all day. I am dying to see you.
Would give worlds that you were here with me at this
moment. I am unhappy, sick—no, not sick, for I am
well, but I am home-sick; sick to be with you. I never
had so great a desire to see you before. I am filled
with thousands of apprehensions. I wonder if you
are perfectly well? I wonder if you love as I know
you have loved? I wonder if any one has attempted
to influence you, that you should for one moment forget your own darling Harry? Oh, dear, dear, sweet,
sweet love! how very, very unhappy I am, and have
been. I cannot divine the cause. It may be without
reason; it may be that I shall never know the reason;
and it may be that I am unhappy without any suffi-
cient cause And yet that cannot be, for you are not
now with me—you could not be. Enough! I am
very, very unhappy.

I sail to-morrow for the South; where, I dare not
tell. I am not permitted to tell. Whether for weal

or woe, the future only knows. Oh ! that this unhappy war was ended. I believe I know two people that would be supremely happy. We would again assure each other of the perfect bliss that there is in being near each other ; in seeing, sighing, feeling, and enjoying the presence of each other. We would lock ourselves within, and the world without, and feel and know how intensely do we love. My own dear little one, I am so very anxious to hear from you; it is so very long. All of our letters have been stopped, and it is now four weeks since I have had a letter. Dearest one, what can I say to you? You know I love you; know I am dying to see you, as you are to see me. But all of the future is enveloped in darkness unfathomable—uncertainty. We have left only hope, and we will hope ; and, judging the future from the past, let us feel assured that that future will bring great happiness with it. When I come, you will want to see me, won't you, dear love? You will die and cry to see me, won't you?

Love to your good mother, and tell her to take the best care in the world of you—that is, if she wants my blessing when I come. Again, and again, God bless you, my own dear, darling, sweet little Baby—my Baby.

Your darling

HARRY.

LETTER LXVI.

Small talk—Blows his own trumpet—Shaken by the hand—
Men shed tears—Love and leaden storms—Hope—Baby
talk to Betsy—"Millions of love," etc.

PORT ROYAL, S. C., Feb. 23, 1863.

MY OWN DEAR BABY:

Your dear little letter, of the 9th of January, was
received this morning—seven weeks in getting to me.
Why, my dear Baby, you write as I feel when ten thousands of things go wrong, and I think, and think, and
can't sleep. Then I think of you, and recollect how
happy we have been. Oh! my dear Petite, how sick,
how very sick I am of this infernal war, and my absence
from that little one who is so very, very happy when we
are together. I am constantly and sorely tried. I am
thrown in contact with so much that is vile; so
many men who pretend to be patriots, and who abuse
every trust placed in them. I am too susceptible; I
am too sensitive, too perceptive, too discerning. I
suspect quicker than any one I ever saw, and my suspicions are seldom at fault; and I fear not the highest
more than the lowest, and am brought in contact with
many of high authority.

I have much heavy work, strong contests, but, dear

Baby, I seldom fail. In all having honor and good purpose to guide me, I always make friends. I am not favored by promotion; but all shake me kindly and warmly by the hand, and remember the hard fighting I have done. This is certainly some reward. My men shed tears when I returned, after an absence of two months, and received me with such shouts of enthusiasm that you, my own dear love, would have shed tears with me. My staff officers and men beg me not to expose myself. All swear by me, and really love me. Strange human nature! Only think of it, my own loved one; these men, now twelve thousand in number, are unknown to me. I have one or two about my person who I know to distinguish, and they are all. I know the general officers, and most of the field officers, and there my acquaintance ceases. But we have fought together, where nature and the man shows for itself. There, there could be no disguise. A man is brave, or a coward; a man has resources, or none. This, with a straight, upright course of conduct, the more severe the better, and a man is beloved by his fellow-men.

Dear, dear mistress of my love and heart, you have occupied my dearest memory, when the storm of lead and iron around me raged to that extent that I thought it impossible to escape. No one who saw me ever imagined it possible to do so. All said I had a charmed life! In you, my Baby, in your love, so entire, devoted, sincere, holy, faithful love, was my life a charmed one. I am now preparing for another contest. Long before you receive this, I shall have succeeded, and Charleston will have fallen; or it may be that we may fail, and your own darling may fall.

I would not write this did I not know that the tele-
graph will announce my fate, if it should be a disas-
trous one. I have no misgivings; on the contrary, I
am full of hope. I exert myself constantly; no one
more than I do, and all with whom I am connected
acknowledge it. I have just finished an ugly correspondence with General Hunter, which is now attract-
ing considerable attention, and in which I have deci-
dedly all the advantage.

Baby, you and I never had any controversy. Ours
has been love, love, love, first and last, and all the
time. You did scold me on several occasions, but I
have forgotten the cause. What was it? Whatever it
was, it was one that showed an excess of love, and
not a want of any. What shall I do, if I should dis-
cover that you do not love me? What should I do
if I was informed that you were unfaithful to me? But
no, your honor would advise me of the change, and I
would be spared. Millions of love to your mother,
and ten times as much to my own sweet, sweet, sweet-
sweet.

HARRY.

LETTER LXVII.

A "sweet, dear little letter"—Hates the "powers that be"—
Gen. Hunter—Wants the "letter" kept secret—"Do you
long for me?" etc.

NEWBERN, N. C., April 19th, 1863.

MY DEAREST LOVE:

I received your sweet, dear little letter; it was brim
full of love and affection, and it made my heart very,
very glad. I have been very sick, and am yet quite
unwell—not suffering, but I have no energy—I am
weak and spiritless. When you are left entirely alone
I am very unhappy. I wish everything was in more
satisfactory condition. I am heartily disgusted with
the "powers that be," and hate them with all my
heart—they have, in the late contest between myself
and General Hunter, treated me most shamefully;
but I have the record clear, and at some time the
truth will be known. All my friends are charmed
that I left the Department of South Carolina. You
don't know how very much I want to see you. We
may well anticipate much happiness, and joy, and
excessive pleasure when next our lips, and eyes, and
arms, and hearts, and souls all commingle in most
exquisite sympathy. Won't you be happy?—'tis worth

much pain to enjoy the contrast of pleasure made the more intense by separation. Don't tell anybody, nor show our letters, will you, love? Do you long for me, and my embrace, and once more to be completely enfolded in my arms? But I .must close. I will write again soon. Love to your mother. I dreamed that your mining stock had a fictitious value.

God bless you. With infinite love and devotion, I am your own darling

HARRY.

LETTER LXVIII.

Small talk—Gen. Foster—Sentiment, etc.

NEWBERN, N. C., April 29th, 1863.

MY DEAR LITTLE ONE:

I wrote to you a few days since, and having a moment whilst waiting my breakfast, I will devote it to her I believe thinks of me always, and loves me always, and dreams and sighs for me always. I am gratified to tell you that I have recovered from extreme illness, and I shall go North in a few days to recruit my health, which I begin to believe has been much injured by constant exposure and excitement, and intense application. I admit that I should not have come so soon from Philadelphia, where my sisters and friends were taking care of me; but Gen. Foster was in a bad scrape, and I considered it my duty to come to his relief. My own darling love, of whom I have so many soft, sweet, delicious memories—of whom, I believe, the angels could not say a word regarding her fidelity to me—who so fully appreciates and acknowledges my friendship and love—who has been made so happy, so very, so exquisitely happy—who was taught to love and be beloved in my embrace. Why, little one, I remember every pulsation of your heart, and every sigh of prolonged love and pleasure. I cannot tell you how much I am dying to see you, and to have peace and rest in your arms. I receive your dear little letters with kisses always, and they always renew the desire to be with you. Love to your mother and your uncle; and I am sincerely, devotedly, lovingly, wholly thy

HARRY.

LETTER LXIX.

A letter—The Administration—The dangers of the situation—
A blast against Lincoln, Stanton, Halleck and Hooker.

PHILADELPHIA, June 26th, 1863.

MY DARLING BABY:

You sweet little plaintive letter was just received, in which you complain that you had not heard from me for a long time. Now, Baby, this is not my fault; I recollect writing to you frequently—not less frequent than once every two weeks. Whether my letters have been captured by the pirates or the Indians, of course, I do not know; because of the latter, I had directed my letters by the steamer; but now, because of the former, I shall be compelled again to try the stage. I am very glad that my lessons of philosophy were not forgotten. I cannot tell you how much I am disgusted with the weakness of the present Adminstration. The rebels are in Pennsylvania, and now threaten the Capital, and will destroy Pittsburg, and yet all is indifference, and an apathy is manifested that surprises everybody. My hope is, that when the flames are seen at Harrisburg, and the explosions heard from the destruction at Pittsburg, that the people will wake up, and arm for the purpose of driving the

invaders back from the North.   But what, in the name
of heaven, can you expect from Lincoln, Stanton,
Halleck and Hooker? I go to Fort Monroe to-
morrow. My health is much recovered. Much love to
your mother—and I am wholly, devotedly,

Your

HARRY.

LETTER LXX.

The "war horse" in the "dumps"—The War Department—
General Grant—The "Nigger"—Remarks—Vicksburg—
"Dream of me"—Some account of himself, etc.

PHILADELPHIA, September 29th, 1863.

MY DEAR BABY:

I received a sweet little letter from you a day or two
since, in which you tell me how very, very much you
want to love me. Alas! my dear child, I am utterly
without hope; I do not see a particle of light in the
future.

I am again the mark of the especial spite of the War
Department, and am now on my way to Vicksburg to
report to Gen. Grant. I inclose you the parting farewell
at Norfolk, by which you will see that I have already
made many friends. Indeed, that was the cause of
the order. I was becoming too well liked; too much
influence. I regret it much, for they will suffer. The
nigger is the constant thought of the Administration,
and complaint was made that I required the negroes
to be out of the street by nine o'clock, and that I put
two regiments of colored troops to work, and returned
two white regiments. I hardly think any policy or
punishment they may adopt will make me prefer a
negro to a white man.

Dear Baby, I am disgusted, and somewhat discouraged; but under no circumstances will I give up. The States must not be separated. War must go on. The revolution and abolition must be put down together. This I believe to be the feeling of the entire country; and the Almighty, I hope, will bring around these results. My dear, sweet, charming little sweetheart, keep up your courage; fear not but there is some good time in the future. I am exceeding sorry to know you are desponding. Why should you be more so than I am? My life is one of exceeding labor and responsibility, with no thanks from the Government I have served most faithfully. I shall leave here in two days, and in ten shall be below Vicksburg. Address me as before. I am encouraged when I read of your love, and feel happy when I know you constantly dream of me. Withal, dear Baby, I am making hosts of friends. All acknowledge the complete, thorough manner I do my business; and discipline, wherever I go, is sure to follow. I have the reputation of being a thorough soldier, and could I only have played the hypocrite, and upheld the negro Government, I could have been very prominent in the army. But, Baby, I not only could not do that, but I could not and would not conceal my utter abhorrence and disgust; the result of which is, that I have been incessantly persecuted. I love opposition; there is an excitement in it.

God bless you. Love on, dear, dear Baby, it will preserve you from evil. Love to your mother, and others; and I am,

Your own dear

HARRY.

LETTER LXXI.

Unwell—"Dear Betsy"—The war—Believes in a Democratic
Government—A smother of "sweet kisses," etc.

CINCINNATI, October 12th, 1863.

MY OWN DEAR, DEAR BABY:

I still await orders from General Grant. I find
myself to-day quite unwell, and very lonely. 'Tis
raining, and having no letter from you for some time,
I thought I could not do a more commendable act
than to write to your own dear self; first, it will render
me more content, and then you, my dear Baby, will be
made happy to know that I always think of you.
How I wish I could tell you so now. How I wish I
could turn the key, and make you feel how much, how
very much I love—and could make you acknowledge
it. Do you still dream of me, dear Betsy? Do you
still dwell with fond remembrance on the past, and
sigh for the future? Do you believe ever lovers were
more happy in heart, and soul, and sympathy?

The war still drags its heavy weight along; changes
continually are made; officers in high rank and favor
to-day are prostrate to-morrow. I am perfectly content with my position; not favored, certainly, by the
Government, but I believe universally respected by

everybody, not excepting those I have offended. I only hope the war will soon be determined. If we had a Democratic Government, it could be stopped at once; without it we will fight for another twelve months; and then, if the Abolitionists again prevail, the Lord only knows when it will end. I am tired of it, but still find determination to do any duty to which I may be assigned.

God bless you, my only dear little sweet one. I am dying to smother you with sweet kisses, long kisses, and sweeter embraces. Love to your good mother, and everybody that loves you and that you love; and am thy

HARRY.

LETTER LXXII.

Love—Indifference—Cold—Sufferings of the troops—Santiago
—Picture—Social matters—"Ten thousands of kisses,"
etc.

CINCINNATI, November 1st, 1863.

MY OWN DARLING BABY:

I hardly know what to say. I have absolutely nothing to tell you, except only that I love you constantly;
that I have the most intense desire to see and be with
you, to make you, if possible, more excessively happy
than ever. I want again to feel that sweet, dear little
heart against mine, and to hear you once breathe, in
flattering words : Dear, dear, darling Harry, how very,
very excessively, excessively happy we are; we were
made indeed for each other.

As to my fate or destiny here, I have become very
indifferent. I am ready to fight, or I am ready not
to fight; but I am not indifferent to our great desire
to be together. I am anxiously awaiting another loving letter, full, brimfull of expression, full, brimfull of
desire to be with him only who ever knew you as you
should be known. We were made for each other, and
will never be happy until we can breathe each to the
other how fully we know and feel the truth of it.

It has been excessively cold, and I need be well contented that my hard usage accidentally favored me. The troops suffered very much ; the cold was intense. I read your slip concerning the Santiago with much interest, and regret that many of my friends were so coolly swindled. They, however, admit they could make the loss without inconvenience, and therefore let us hope they will keep the money they have left. It is sometimes almost as troublesome to have too much money as to have too little.

I look at the picture constantly, and as often say to myself, how very, very happy will she be when she again clasps me to her own dear little sweet self. I can give you no definite idea of my future movements, but will advise you of every change. Your letters are always sent to me by my correspondent in Philadelphia, who is always advised of my address. Give my love to that excellent old lady who is, next to my Baby, the dearest old lady in the world. Dear darling, ten thousands of kisses await you, and a certainty which you must always feel, that I shall do all in my power to make you always happy. Love, dear, dear, sweet Baby, love !

HARRY.

LETTER LXXIII.

"Reminders"—Love-smitten—The War—Military uncertainty,
etc., etc.

CINCINNATI, November 15th, 1863.

MY OWN DEAR, DEAR LITTLE ONE:

Two sweet little reminders came so opportunely,
that my convalescence was turned to a complete cure.
I have not felt so well for twelve months. The letter
was filled with warm expressions of true, pure love,
gushing fresh and warm from a truly-loving little
heart; and the picture was so like her dear self, and
reminded me of so many endearing moments of exquisite happiness, that I find myself constantly sighing—constantly absorbed—constantly unhappy that
we are not together. Doing nothing—the contrast
with the constant labor so lately required of me—the
absence of the malarious influences removed by late
severe illness—the receipt of your sweet, charming,
dear letter has sent a thrill through me that fills me
with the most tender love and desire for you, and I
am really miserable that we cannot be made supremely
happy. Oh! dearest, fondest·one—oh! cruel neces-

sity—oh! wretched uncertainty—oh! that two made
so expressly for each other, should sigh, and pine, and
die with desire.

I have written to you quite often—always when
less occupied. My memory floats back to you and
yours — to thine and mine, and mine and thine.
Well, dearest Baby, think and dream of me; remember that the ties that have so often held us breathlessly bound, heart and soul, and body, control our
existence—control our destiny—memory will not forget
the past, and hope will certainly secure the future.
The war is assuming a new shape, and I shall be much
surprised if it does not soon end. The South are
nearly exhausted. The people are becoming sick of
so much suffering. The North, on the contrary, are
preparing a stronger and better force than at any past
moment. Let the war end, that our love may again
begin. I don't know, my dear Baby, how to advise
you about your business at Baltimore. I know nothing
of the nature of the case, and until fully advised, I
would not like to make up any opinion. Indeed,
without full information, my opinion would be worth-
less. One thing I know, however, and of that I
need not assure my dear Baby, that if I can in any
manner assist her, or her good old mother, I am
always ready. My future is so very, very uncertain.
I am awaiting orders from Gen. Grant, which may come
at any moment, and may order me to Vicksburg, or to
any point within Tennessee, Kentucky, Mississippi,
Ohio or Missouri; or he may leave me here, doing
nothing. I shall advise you of any change, and shall
continue to love and dream about you, and to burn up

with a consuming desire to love you. Much love to
your mother—and am truly, devotedly, lovingly,
Thy own darling

HARRY.

Three cent (3) stamp is all now necessary for
postage.

LETTER LXXIV.

Kisses a picture — The "war horse" desperate — Love and
philosophy—Kisses in thousands, etc.

PHILADELPHIA, December 20th, 1863.

MY OWN DEAR BABY:

What shall I say? How can I tell you how I have
been making a perfect Judy of myself? Here have I
been for half an hour straining my eyes, and kissing
and smiling—and kissing a sweet, dear, precious little
picture. It is excellent—it is herself. Oh! my dear
one, it has set me more in love with you than ever,
and my impatience is growing to that extreme, that
you to me will come, or I to you will go. I must
have you heart to heart—body to body—soul and
body, heart, arms and all so closely interwined, that
to separate us, or even to know which was which, or
which belonged to the other, would be difficult. Are
you, dear, sweet one, as kind, affectionate, lovely and
loving as your picture indicates? Can you still· and
always hold on to your old war horse, so far away
from you, when there are so many prancing, gay
ponies *"gallivanting"* constantly near and around
you? Oh! dear, dear, lovely little one, with my entire
heart and soul I do so truly and entirely find myself

absorbed in my remembrances and love of you. Ours
has been a kind, affectionate, happy love. It commenced in rain and darkness, but it was a generous
gift on your part, and generously and happily received
on mine. It continued, and oh! how happy was the
history of it—it still continues, spite of all the trials
of a cruel, unhappy, miserable separation; but I
believe it increases with the obstacles thrown between
us. My own dear, dear Baby, oh! how much and
how dearly do we love. Again am I looking, and
intently gazing. The eyes seem to reproach me, that
it has been so very long that I have not held your
heart to mine. The lips seem about to reproach me,
that their sweet honey had not been sipped by their
companions, and that bosom seems raised, filled, with
anguish and a constant hope in the promise of the
future.

Oh! dear, dear Baby, 'tis cruel, 'tis misery, indeed.
But our destiny is fixed, and let us hope, the trial is
nearly over. The war will, I really believe, soon be
over; and then—yes, loved one—then will we forget
the past in the present and the future. Again, and
again, thousands of kisses — long, sweet, thrilling
kisses—kisses known to none save you and I. My
love to your excellent, good mother. I am here for a
day to attend to some important business, and I shall
return in two or three days—sweet, dear, charming
one—love—love—love—ever,

HARRY.

LETTER LXXV.

Family affairs—Kisses—Government officials—Love to all, etc.

PHILADELPHIA, February 24th, 1864.

MY DEAR DARLING BABY :

I feel quite sure you expect a letter, and that you begin to grow a little nervous. I have but little to say that is new, a mere repetition of the same story ignored—doing nothing ; pretty well ; merely living, waiting the future. I have been here for two weeks ; go West to-night. Have been here with the purpose of a partition of my father's estate, but the lawyers opposed to me have succeeded in putting the subject off until March, and I must obey.

Well, my dear little love, are you still as loving, and sweet, and fresh, and blooming, and plump, and as full of desire to see and feel your Harry as ever? What a long history you will have to recount, and how many kisses will be given and received to square the account, accumulated through so long an absence. We will only promise they shall be the longer and sweeter, and the more full of feeling—warm, gushing, full of joy and passion, directly from the heart. I am tired of the war ; I am tired of being separated from your close embrace. I want the repose of my country home. I want to get out of the way of all Government officials, who stink of corruption, and of their foul association. I am tired of living and being governed by men who shrink from an honest man, and whose acts are all so foul that they are constantly in dread of being exposed.

But withal, dear little one, courage, courage ! Let us live with the hope that all will be well ; that the wheel will turn, and that this abundance of villainy will meet with its just punishment. Give my love to your good mother : and regards to * * * , and love, and esteem, and affection, and kisses innumerable, for my Baby.

HARRY.

LETTER LXXVI.

Out of service—Lincoln Administration—Small talk, etc.

PHILADELPHIA, April 19th, 1864.

'MY DEAR BABY:

You will have heard before this of my being no longer in the army. Without a word of explanation, without any justification, I have been dropped from the rolls of the army, and all because, despite all threats or offers of reward, I would not abandon my principles—I would not be abolitionized. I thank God, my self-respect feels elevated. I feel that I am not serving an Administration who will destroy all of the constitutional guaranties, and do any and everything to continue their infamous and ruinous rôle. I now await the developments of the coming sixty days, prepared for the worst, for the future rests upon mere chance. I am prepared for success or defeat, and with the latter, ruin or revolution in the North. The most extraordinary distrust, and want of confidence—all feel the weakness and imbecility of the Lincoln Administration, and feel that we are drifting, without a single guiding hand to foretell or understand our position. I shall write again soon.

and may determine very suddenly to come to quiet and repose, and you. Give my love to your mother; and as ever, with very much love, I am

Your

HARRY.

LETTER LXXVII.

A letter—Heavy losses—Happiness anticipated—Movements, etc.

PHILADELPHIA, May 12th, 1864.

MY OWN BABY:

Your sweet little favor was received a few days since, and reminds me that you will again be nervous and restless unless you are again assured of my devotion and love. I advised you that I had been dropped from the army, because I would not be abolitionized, and because I would expose the weakness of the Government. It is just as well, for it may save me from a rebel bullet, and insure our meeting at a much earlier moment than it would otherwise have been. I wait now to see the termination of the awful carnage that is now going on in the Army of the Potomac, and which, unless it be proportionately severe with the enemy, must soon destroy our army. In the week's fighting, Grant has lost forty to fifty thousand men. Will you be glad to see me? Will you receive me with open arms? And will you make me very, very happy? Yes! My dear Baby, I shall come back with infinite satisfaction, and shall be only too happy to find the repose, the rest of mind, and absence of excitement, now become absolutely necessary. I shall keep you advised of my movements, and will not take you too much by surprise. Give my love to your mother; and with kisses and love,

I am wholly thy

HARRY.

LETTER LXXVIII.

Fighting—Butler—Politics—Political prospects—Sentiment—
Medicine, etc.

PHILADELPHIA, May 20th, 1864.

MY DEAR BABY:

The severe fighting and great losses of the past
three weeks have as yet produced no definite result.
The armies are in very close position, and the fighting
will commence again soon.   Butler—the Beast—has
been very badly beaten, and Sigel has been treated
in the same way.   All are very anxiously looking
upon the Army of the Potomac, all feeling that much
of the future depends upon it.   The political future
will entirely be governed by success or defeat in that
direction.

I hear you say, you don't care for politics, and the
political future.   But, my dear Baby, our happiness
will much depend upon it.   If Lincoln is elected, I
fear the excessive, now arbitrary, will no longer be
borne, and that there may be a revolution in the
North ; and then we will have misery and ruin such
as none have yet seen or dreamed of.

I hope, my dear little one, to find you soon, and to
find you all I can and do desire to find you—amia-

ble, and sweet, and kind, and happy, and in perfect health. What change may I expect in so long an absence, and how very, very happy you will be, are subjects of constant thought. I shall advise you of my coming, yet undetermined, for so much must be determined soon, that I cannot turn my back upon the vastly important issue so soon to be made known. I have not been well, and have been taking medicine. Give my love to your mother and uncle * * * ; and for yourself, oceans of love, kisses, and close embraces.

LETTER LXXIX.

"Sweet favor"—Devotion—Sickness—The "grand Issue"—
Election—Love—Gen. McClellan, etc.

PHILADELPHIA, July 25th, 1864.

MY DEAR BABY:

Your sweet little favor of the 30th June is now before me, and appeals so directly to my heart, that I will not delay the response a single moment. I cannot fix the day of my departure, but, as I have advised you, will be only too happy when I can tell you to expect me. That you love me, dear Baby, tenderly, I believe it most sincerely. Why should I believe otherwise? I have been certainly always deserving of your constant, devoted, entire love, and you have always assured me that I possessed it fully, freely, voluntarily, and that you were most happy that it were so.

My own dear Baby, I have been in bed for four days with an attack of diarrhœa and congestion of the liver, but am now out and much better. It is the constantly recurrent disease contracted on the Peninsula. I await the grand issue—the nominations of August and the elections of November. This nation lives or does not live after they shall have passed. A strong suspicion exists that it is the intention of the present Government to continue in power by the force of the bayonet, regardless of all the elections, and that an effort will be made to force the elections. Do, dear Baby, live along, alone, a little longer—you will love me none the less when at last I come to claim what you propose, and that you will then convince me of the intensity of your love.

I am identified with Gen. McClellan ; we have been treated with outrage and insult, when we were entitled to thanks and consideration.

But it is an unpleasant subject, and I want to remind you only of the most agreeable ones—of our love—of our desires to be again together, and to be happy.

God bless you, my dear little Baby.

HARRY,

LETTER LXXX.

Melancholy—Slaughter—" Glad to be out of the way"—Private affairs—Maladies—Expectations, etc.

PHILADELPHIA, Nov. 15th, 1864.

MY DEAR PETITE:

I received your very little favor but a few days since. It relieved me of much solicitude, for I had imagined you ill, or *married*, or gone to China or Australia, or to some other foreign place. At last the day is fixed for my departure, and the third of December rapidly draws nigh. I look upon the future with a heart full of sadness. I can see nothing but dark, black, gloomy results, that must come from the policy of this Administration. The war will go on for the purpose of extermination, and this will increase its bitterness and cruelty. There will be dreadful slaughter, and no friendly hand will be allowed to interfere.

The coming two years will try the country and this people, and there will be an awful crisis. I shall only be too happy to be out of the way. If I cannot be permitted to save, I will not be a party to assist in the destruction.

I have some forebodings that my private affairs are

in some difficulty, and regret that that will mar the anticipated quiet and repose that I so much desire. But with Mickel and other kind friends, I hope to get it into shape, and avoid long complication. I am quite unwell. I have been suffering the pains intense from a boil on the end of my nose, and my head distresses me beyond measure. I do not know any Colonel, such as that Vestal has recognized as an intimate friend. He is an impostor. Will you be glad to see me? I shall arrive in the *Constitution*, about the end of December. Give my love to your mother and uncle * * * , and await my coming, full of affection and love.

LARRY.

LETTER LXXXI.

He gives her a "square shake" and the "cold shoulder."

MY DEAR FRIEND:

I have been quite unwell since my arrival, but not ill enough to be confined to my room. I have not called again, for the reason that I have no intention to interrupt any of your friendly associations so agreeably established.

I shall always be most happy to know that you are doing well.

Truly, yours,

HARRY.

CPSIA information can be obtained at www.ICGtesting.com
Printed in the USA
BVOW042133270613

324504BV00010B/306/P